DISCOVERING THE PSALMS

PASSION, PROMISE & PRAISE

LEADER'S GUIDE

Donald L. Griggs

the KERYGMA
program

Discovering the Psalms: Passion, Promise & Praise is published and distributed by The Kerygma Program, Suite 205, 300 Mt. Lebanon Boulevard, Pittsburgh, PA 15234. Phone 800/537-9462. FAX 412/344-1823.

Cover design by Kathy Boykowycz

ISBN 1-882236-17-3

Suite 205
300 Mt. Lebanon Boulevard
Pittsburgh, PA 15234
800/537-9462

CONTENTS

A LOOK AT THE COURSE

The Leader

You are most likely reading this *Leader's Guide* because you are considering the possibility of, or have already committed yourself to, leading a group of participants in a creative approach to studying the Psalms. Whether you are a clergy person, a church educator, or a lay person, it is less important how much you remember about your previous study of Psalms than that you are now willing to engage in an intensive process of reading, studying, planning, and leading. There are no short cuts to a successful study of the Bible using the Kerygma approach. It will require a significant commitment of time and energy in order to share effective session plans with those who are engaged in this study with you.

As a leader of a Kerygma Bible study group, you will function in a variety of roles at different times. You are first of all a *learner*. Being a Kerygma leader may be the best opportunity for learning more about this wonderful book of the Bible. You are not expected to be an expert teacher of the biblical material on which the course is based. However, you are expected to be prepared for each session so that you are able to guide the members of the group in a productive study.

As a result of all the reading in preparation for leading each session, you will also become a *resource person*. You are not expected to know all the answers to every question that is raised, but you should be able to direct group members to resources that will assist them to find answers for themselves.

Furthermore, you will be a *planner* who works intentionally to consider session plan suggestions, the time available, the needs, interests, and abilities of the participants, and the resources available in order to develop an appropriate plan for each session. The session plans offered in this *Leader's Guide* are very complete and probably offer more than you will be able to accomplish in the time you have. However, the best session plan is the one you construct using the suggestions here as well as your own personal resources and experiences.

Being a *facilitator* of group process is also a very important role for you to perform. The seven session plans include many activities that involve participants in processes of investigation, discussion, reflection, creativity, and application. The more comfortable you become in guiding group process, the more effective the study will be for others. At first, some participants may prefer having you tell them what they should know about the psalm type or a particular psalm. And, there are times when you may be tempted to tell them all that you know. However, you will be most effective as a leader and the group will gain most from the course when they are guided by you in a variety of participatory activities as you explore Psalms together.

Throughout the course of study you will also be called upon to exercise several important qualities. With the constraint of time and the great body of material to explore, you must be *flexible*. Unplanned questions will arise, activities will take longer than anticipated, and participants may want to go slower than you feel is necessary. In addition, you will need to be *patient* with the author when the written material is confusing or unclear. Unprepared participants will also test your patience. And, unpredictable occurrences in the life of the group and the church will require patience.

Those Who Participate in Kerygma Groups

The people who choose to associate with a group that is studying the Bible using the Kerygma resources and approach do so for a variety of motives and bring with them many levels of readiness and ability. When individuals are invited to attend a Kerygma group, they should be made aware from the beginning that this is not a study of the Bible where the leader does all the work of preparation and presentation. Every participant is expected to have read the Basic Bible References and the appropriate material in the *Resource Book* prior to each session. Familiarity with this material is assumed by the session plans that are developed in the *Leader's Guide*.

Given the busy schedules of most people, there will be times when some come to a session with minimum preparation. You should not compromise the expectation of adequate preparation, because the experience for the whole group will suffer if the reading is not taken seriously. There are several ways you can handle the lack of preparation by the participants.

1. Encourage persons who have not read the assignments not to participate in the discussion until others have had a chance.

2. Provide some time, as a part of the session plan, to review the key texts that serve as the foundation for the session.

3. When working in pairs or small groups, be sure that those who are not prepared are distributed among the groups rather than being grouped together.

Some participants will have had a lot of experience with Psalms, but for others this will be their first experience to be involved in an in-depth study of this book as adults. It is important for each person to feel that he or she belongs to the group. You will need to encourage both the experienced and inexperienced participants to be mindful and appreciative of each other.

Number of Sessions and Amount of Time

When planning to offer a course such as this it is important to ask and answer several key questions such as: How will this study fit into our adult education program? How many weeks or sessions will we schedule? How much time should be planned for each session? Perhaps those questions have already been answered in your church and necessary arrangements have been made. If so, you and your group will have to adjust to what is already planned. However, if the questions have not been answered, you may want to consider a variety of options. There are leadership strategies for seven sessions. However, there are several ways to adjust the scheduling of those seven sessions: a) Seven sessions of two hours each could be planned. The materials will work very well in this format. b) If you are planning to offer the course during the six weeks of Lent, then one session could be omitted. However, do no omit session one. c) You can plan for the course to go for thirteen or fourteen weeks with one hour per session. There is enough material to stretch the course out but it will take some adapting on the part of the leader for each session to be complete with Setting the Stage, Exploring the Scripture, and Closing. d) If the leader of the group has sufficient familiarity with Psalms and additional resources, it is possible to use this course as a basis for building a longer course in which the leader will incorporate his or her own knowledge, expertise, and creativity.

The Bible

The major curricular resource for *Discovering the Psalms* is the Bible. The New Revised Standard Version of the Bible is the translation on which this course is based. However, participants will be able to engage in the study effectively with another translation. In fact, the study is enhanced by the presence of several translations. A study Bible, with notes for each psalm and other study aids, is recommended for the leader as well as the participants. Among those containing good study notes are the *New Oxford Annotated Bible with Apocrypha: NRSV. The Oxford Study Bible with Apocrypha*, and the *New Jerusalem Bible (with complete notes)*. In the *Resource Book* we suggest that participants may want to read and study Psalms for this course with two Bibles, one which is their favorite or most familiar and one which is a different or newer translation.

Discovering the Psalms *Resource Book*

The *Resource Book* is a guide to reading and exploring selected psalms each week. This is the text that both leaders and participants will use to guide their study. There are six to ten pages of text for each part, with all the related Psalms passages identified clearly. This volume contains all the necessary information for the entire study to enable persons to participate responsibly in the group sessions.

As you review the *Resource Book,* you will note that each part begins with a Summary and includes a listing of Basic Bible References and a Word List. In the main body of the text, the Basic Bible References are in boldface type. As a leader, you should read the *Resource Book* from beginning to end before you start planning any particular sessions. This effort will provide you with an overview of the total study. As you then plan for each session, you will need to reread the appropriate material for that session.

There are three other features of the *Resource Book* that are different in this study than other Kerygma courses. Each of these features reflects the unique nature of Psalms as devotional literature. 1) Before the main body of the text, verses of a psalm are included. This section is called "Praying with the Psalmist." In Part 1 there are some suggestions as to how the participants can incorporate these prayers into their weekly devotions and preparation. 2) The main body of the text also concludes with selected verses of a psalm which are offered as a "Closing Prayer." The opening and closing prayers are related to the topic of the part. 3) Each part concludes with a section, "Reading Psalms for "Devotions and Study." Except for Part 1, one psalm is suggested for reading and reflecting each day. These psalms are usually included among the Basic Bible References. If participants are able to spend some time each day reading the selected psalm plus other material in the *Resource Book* they will be well prepared for each week's group session.

Discovering the Psalms *Leader's Guide*

This is the book you have in your hands at this moment. It will be the indispensable resource you will use for planning each session. You will notice that the *Leader's Guide* contains detailed suggestions for guiding each of the seven parts.

Each of the parts includes:

1. **Background from the Author** provides background information on the focus of that part. Also included are helpful comments on ways of dealing with various aspects of the session plans.

2. **Session Plans:** Extensive suggestions for session planning are provided for each part. Kerygma Bible study groups have been successfully led with the lecture and discussion format as well as where the emphasis was on participatory activities. There is, however, overwhelming evidence that adult learning is increased and enhanced when group members participate directly in the learning process. It is strongly recommended that all leaders review the session plans and incorporate as many suggestions as appropriate into each session. The session plans in the *Leader's Guide* include:

    a. **Learning Objectives**: The three or four statements presenting the learning objectives indicate what the leader will help the participants to accomplish as a result of their study. It is appropriate to share these objectives with the members of the group at the beginning of each session. The selection of activities is then guided by the objectives considered most important. The statements of learning objectives can also be used as a basis for evaluating whether or not you and the participants have accomplished what was intended. A word of caution: Accomplishing the learning objectives is not all there is to leading a Kerygma Bible study group. Some of the most important things that happen among participants in a Kerygma group cannot be evaluated by learning objectives: Forming Christian community, growing in faith, developing the ability to speak comfortably about one's faith, nurturing the spiritual life as well as other important matters regarding the Christian faith and life.

    b. **Resources:** In addition to a Bible, the *Resource Book,* and supplementary reading, a list of those resources that are needed for the various activities is provided.

c. **Leadership Strategy:** This is the heart of the session plan. The leadership strategy is organized in three sections. Setting the Stage is a time for engaging participants in prayer, prompted by one or more psalms, and inviting them to become involved with the subject of the session. Ordinarily it will take 10-15 minutes for this section. Exploring the Scripture is what the study is about. Most of the time of the session will be spent with activities that enable exploration of this material. Usually three or more activities will be planned for this portion of the session. Closing is a time to bring closure to the session, to summarize what has been explored, and to make applications of what has been learned to one's own faith and life experiences.

d. **Supplementary Readings:** To provide access to background material relevant to the biblical texts referred to in the *Resource Book,* references to Bible dictionaries and commentaries are often listed. In addition, one key book on Psalms is referred to frequently. It is *Out of the Depths: The Psalms Speak for Us Today* by Bernard Anderson. Leaders will find this to be a helpful resource as they prepare for each session. Specific chapters or pages, appropriate to each part, are indicated.

e. **Looking Ahead:** In order to work effectively in the next session, some special tasks may need preparation by some or all of the participants. For example, occasionally a brief report requiring advance preparation is called for. Participants are invited to volunteer for these assignments. Of course, the basic assignment for each week is reading the *Resource Book* and the Basic Bible References.

Praying Prompted by the Psalmists

You will notice that each of the seven sessions begins and ends with a way of praying together prompted by several verses from a psalm. We will experience a variety of models of praying the psalms. If you have not led groups in this way of praying prompted by Scripture you will discover that most members of the group will respond very positively to the process. All of the praying activities have been tried, tested and revised so that you can be assured they will work with your group. Though there will be a variety of praying the psalms activities, they all have several common features: 1) They involve everyone; 2) they seek to connect ancient psalms with the present reality of a person's life; 3) they engage the participants in dialogue with God as well as with the psalmist; and 4) they allow individuals to respond personally in their own ways. As leader, make the activities your own so that you are comfortable with them, but stay as close to the plan as you can. My advice is not to change the activities significantly until you have tried them and discover that a particular model does not work for you and/or your group.

You are about to embark on a wonderful journey with a number of companions. This time together has the potential for building relationships among those who participate, for increasing their knowledge and appreciation of Psalms, for providing a time of spiritual nurture and renewal which many yearn for, and for leading members of your group to desire to participate in other Bible study groups using Kerygma courses or other quality resources. All of the study is for naught if it does not lead persons to increased commitment to love and serve God, to live as faithful disciples of Jesus Christ, and to engage in the larger mission of the Church. May this be a fruitful time of study and reflection for you and those who join you on the journey.

PART ONE

THE BOOK OF PSALMS: AN OVERVIEW

BACKGROUND FROM THE AUTHOR

With this session we begin the adventure of exploring the Psalms in order to discover the beauty, wisdom, and power of this wonderful book for God's people throughout the ages as well as for our lives today. No doubt you as leader, as well as the participants in your group, are familiar with Psalms and find it to be a great inspiration and influence in your spiritual journey. There are several ways we could approach an in-depth study of the book. One way is to take a historical-critical approach and consider the views of various biblical scholars, drawing upon their careful analyses of the whole collection as well as individual literary pieces. Another way is to approach the psalms as great examples of religious literature. A third way is to come to the psalms devotionally, reading and reflecting on them to receive and share whatever inspiration and insight will nurture our spiritual selves. Or we could deal with the psalms one at a time, focusing on our favorites or on those that show promise to provide for a most fruitful study. In this course we will combine aspects of all these approaches.

We approach Psalms with some familiarity. Yet, many members of the group will not be aware of all the important details that contribute to a greater appreciation and under-standing of the book as a whole and of individual psalms. This session and the next, more than the other five, will focus on many of these general details. It is true that Psalms can be appreciated without much attention to such information. However, when persons become familiar with the details, they will be able to read and pray the psalms with more awareness and sensitivity to the richness present in these deep expressions of faith in God.

As you work with the group in the first half of this session, looking at several distin-guishing features of Psalms, be sensitive to the participants' levels of interest in the details. Don't spend so much time on the process that participants become overwhelmed.

Try to help them feel that they are engaged in a "guided tour" of familiar territory where they will be discovering things they may not have noticed before. Be sure to welcome the sharing of impressions and experiences the class members bring with them from previous studies of Psalms and to affirm each one's offerings. Make the review of the details lively and fun.

Something that will help members of the group make new discoveries is for them to read Psalms from a different translation in addition to the one with which they are most familiar. In preparing this course I have used *The New Oxford Annotated Bible: NRSV.* For those in the group who do not have that version of the Bible, recommend that they consider obtaining a copy. (Copies may be purchased from The Kerygma Program office.) They will find it very helpful as they read the *Resource Book* for their weekly preparation. However, it is also important to affirm whatever versions of the Bible people bring to the study group. Take advantage of the several translations and versions which are present for each session; the study will be enhanced considerably by the contributions from various Bibles. A word of caution: If someone has a copy of *The Living Bible* try to persuade him or her to use a different Bible. This paraphrase of Psalms presents them in the form of prose, not poetry. It will not be very helpful for the type of study we will be doing in the course.

In the second half of this session we will identify ten different types of psalms. In the *Resource Book* I have suggested that there are many ways to classify psalms. I have chosen to use the categories suggested in the notes of *The New Oxford Annotated Bible: NRSV.* Be sure to be flexible on this matter. If a different way of classifying one or more psalms is suggested, encourage the participant to say why he or she sees it that way and affirm that there are many ways to identify psalms by types. Depending on which verses one considers, it is often possible to place a psalm in a different category from the one suggested. In the scholarly literature there is much debate about the value of classifying psalms by types. Despite the debate, I continue to find it helpful to recognize that the psalms are not all the same, that some psalms have features in common and that identifying psalms by type helps to unlock some of the specialness of particular psalms.

SESSION PLANS

Learning Objectives

It is intended that this session will enable the participants to:

1. Become acquainted with the others in the group and begin to feel comfortable sharing their ideas, feelings, and experiences related to Psalms.

2. Recognize the place of Psalms in the whole Bible.

3. Describe some of the features of particular psalms that can be seen throughout Psalms.

4. Identify selected psalms according to various literary types.

5. Make connections between the words of psalms and their own journeys of faith.

6. Commit themselves to reading and praying psalms on a daily basis, using a second translation in addition to the one they use regularly.

Resources

The following items will be valuable for leading this session:

Several translations, versions, and paraphrases of Psalms

Participants' Resources - 1A, 1B, 1C, 1D, and 1E

A chalkboard or newsprint easel

Leadership Strategy

Setting the Stage

1. In this first session there are several things that must be accomplished as quickly and effectively as possible so that participants will become comfortable with one another and with the subject of the study. If there is anyone in the group who does not know everyone else, provide name tags and ask the members of the group to introduce themselves. One way to do this is to have each person share his or her name plus one or more of the following:

Why they chose to attend this course.

When they received or purchased the Bible they brought with them.

What they hope to receive from this course.

and

On page 18 you will find Participants' Resource - 1A, "Opening Prayer," with the words of Psalm 95:1-7. You may duplicate copies of the Participants' Resource sheet so that each member of the group will have a copy. This psalm was selected because it is probably familiar to most of the group and it sets a tone of praise and worship. After introducing the psalm lead the group in the prayer. There are several ways to do this: 1) Pray in unison, 2) pray antiphonally with each half of the group reading alternate lines, or 3) read one line at a time and have the group respond each time with *The LORD is a great God!*

or

If all participants have the same translation of the Bible you can lead them in one of the above ways by reading Psalm 95:1-7 directly from the Bible.

2. Invite those who are willing to share some of their experiences with Psalms. Don't pressure someone to share if he or she is unwilling. Instead of going around the circle allow for what I call a "popcorn approach," which means individuals speak up when they are ready. What we are trying to accomplish is to help everyone "get on board" with the subject of Psalms. In this brief time of sharing you, as the leader, will get some clues regarding each of the participant's experiences and familiarity with Psalms. Each person will have had some previous experiences with the book and some interest in it or he or she would not be attending the course. Choose among the following questions, or devise some of your own, to accomplish this purpose of opening up the subject.

Q. What is the first memory you can recall of hearing Psalms?

Q. When can you remember Psalms being used in worship?

Q. Do you recall having memorized a psalm? Which one?

Q. When have you turned to Psalms to read them?

Q. What are some impressions you have of Psalms?

Q. Have you participated in a previous study of Psalms? Describe it.

Instead of having a time of sharing guided by one or more of the above questions it may be just as valuable to invite each participant to share a favorite psalm and to speak very briefly about why it has become a favorite. This activity will be most appropriate if the group is composed of "veteran" Bible readers and you are reasonably assured that everyone will have a favorite psalm.

3. Conclude these opening activities with a few words expressing your joy in the group's interest in studying Psalms. And, speak briefly about your excitement for the course and what you hope will happen in the weekly sessions that you share together.

Exploring the Scripture

1. Refer to some of the things that have been shared in the previous activities in order to move into exploring Psalms in more depth. In this exploring part of the session we will be looking at a number of details regarding the way the Book of Psalms is presented. There are two different approaches you can take. If you have only an hour for your study time you will probably take the first approach. If you have more than an hour or can devote two sessions to this part, try the second approach.

The first approach is more deductive, where you are the "tour guide" leading the group through some of the "byways" of Psalms. Participants' Resource - 1B, "The Psalms," is the one to use for this approach. In this resource I have reproduced a page from Psalms, including all of the elements seen in the NRSV translation. I have noted the points to be made in the presentation with small, bold superscript letters,[a] - [g], on the Participants' Resource sheets. Encourage all participants to keep their own Bibles open so they can see the similarities and differences between their Bibles and what you are presenting.

The information you will need for your remarks can be found on pages 7-10 in the *Resource Book,* or in Chapter 1 of *Out of the Depths.* If the members of the group did not receive their *Resource Books* prior to this session it is all the more necessary to summarize this information carefully.

Introduce the presentation by commenting that you are going to take the group on a "tour of a familiar neighborhood." Together you are going to look closely at some things in Psalms that perhaps they had not noticed before. If the participants received their *Resource Books* ahead of time and have read Part 1, invite them to share something they remember from their reading as you guide them on the "tour." The points to note for each superscript are:

a   The placement of Psalms between Job and Proverbs, as represented by a page number. Speak about Psalms being included in the collection of Writings.

b   The title of the book, Psalms or The Psalms. The Hebrew title is *tehillim*, which means "songs of praise." The Greek psalmos means "a song sung to the accompaniment of stringed instruments."

c   Book I. Comment briefly about the five books of Psalms.

d   The poetic format of psalms. Don't take time to deal with poetry in detail because this will be a major emphasis in Part 2.

e   Look at Psalm 2:11, 12. There are several points to make here: 1) Call attention to the fact that footnotes appear throughout Psalms, 2) parts of verses are referred to as "a" and "b," 3) find the page at the beginning of the Bible that explains the abbreviations "Cn" and "Heb." Psalm 2:11, 12 is an excellent place to compare translations. Since the Hebrew is uncertain for these lines there will be a variety of ways the words are translated. Also see if a similar footnote appears in other translations. A second type of footnote is a cross-reference note, which indicates other places where the same phrase, line, or verse appears in the Bible.

f   Point out the title or superscription of Psalm 3. There are several points to make here: 1) 116 additional psalms have titles, 2) seventy-two psalms are attributed to David, 3) other psalms are attributed to various persons and groups, and 4) thirteen psalms have specific references to events in David's life.

g   Notice the word *Selah* after Psalm 3:2. Review possible meanings for the word mentioned in the *Resource Book* and emphasize that we usually don't say the word aloud.

Invite questions and comments from the group members. However, don't get side-tracked, because there is another major part of the session to be accomplished.

or

The second approach to dealing with the above material is more inductive and will take more time. Distribute copies of Participants' Resource - 1C, "Seven

Significant Details." The participants will work alone or in pairs or small groups to locate the information they need and share their findings with the rest of the group.

There are eight topics to be explored. If you have fewer than eight in your group, each person can take more than one topic. If you have nine to fifteen persons in the group, they can work in pairs with each pair dealing with one or two of the topics. If you have sixteen or more in the group, then they can work in pairs or triads. The groups are to deal only with their assigned topic, and then take notes on the other topics when they are presented in a plenary session.

and

After you have used either of the above approaches spend a few minutes reflecting on the things that have been discovered. Ask the group members what insights they have gained regarding Psalms. Or, ask what new impressions they have of Psalms as a book in the Bible.

2. The second major focus of Part 1 is the classification of psalms by various types. Introduce the topic by using some of the information on pages 10 to 13 of the *Resource Book* and notes found in one or more study Bibles.

After a general introduction, indicate that we are going to focus on ten different psalm types. Distribute copies of Participants' Resource - 1D, "Matching Exercise." Each selection represents a particular type. No trick items are intended. This exercise is not a test, but rather a way for one to start distinguishing between one type of psalm and another. Provide about ten minutes for the group to work in pairs to complete the exercise. Then poll the pairs to compare their selections.

Because of the limited evidence on which to make a judgment (verses rather than complete psalms), limited time, and limited knowledge about psalm types, neither the participants nor the leader should expect a large number of similar matchings. However, it will be helpful for individuals to compare their judgments with one another and to give the reasons for their choices. The answers that I intended, and the key words or phrases that provide clues for the matching are:

1. = Song of Zion . . . city of our God . . . his holy mountain.

2. = Psalm of Lament . . . How long . . . how long . . . how long?

3. = Enthronement Psalm . . . The LORD is a great King above all gods.

4. = Psalm of Trust . . . my hope is from him . . . I shall not be shaken.

5. = Psalm of Praise . . . Make a joyful noise . . . worship with gladness.

6. = Sacred History Psalm . . . Our ancestors . . . wonderful works.

7. = Royal Psalm . . . the king . . .

8. = Liturgy Psalm . . . (an entrance liturgy into the temple.)

9. = Wisdom Psalm . . . (two short proverbs.)

10. = Psalm of Thanksgiving . . . O give thanks . . .

Remember that there may be legitimate differences of opinion, so the "correct" answers may be challenged for good reason. It should take about fifteen minutes to complete the matching exercise and to work as a group to compare choices.

3. After completing the matching exercise, invite the group to work in pairs to practice identifying psalm types using Participants' Resource - 1E, "Searching for Psalm Types." Two psalms are listed for each type. Provide about ten minutes for the pairs to skim two to four psalms and determine which types they represent. If possible, divide the whole list among the group so that all psalms are dealt with. After the pairs complete their work, take another ten minutes to review what they have decided.

The psalms on the list by type are:

1.	Hymns of Praise	Psalms 66 and 111
2.	Enthronement Psalms	Psalms 47 and 95
3.	Songs of Zion	Psalms 76 and 87
4.	Psalms of Lament	Psalms 12 and 42
5.	Songs of Trust	Psalms 23 and 121
6.	Sacred History Psalms	Psalms 105 and 136
7.	Royal Psalms	Psalms 20 and 72
8.	Songs of Thanksgiving	Psalms 30 and 92
9.	Wisdom Psalms	Psalms 1 and 119
10.	Liturgies	Psalms 15 and 122

or

If you have less than twenty minutes for the above activity, take the lead and work with one psalm at a time from each of the ten categories on Participants' Resource - 1E. Of course you will need to prepare ahead of time by identifying the key words, phrases, or verses of each psalm that are the clues to its classification. Invite the participants to look for these clues in each psalm. Later they can use Participants' Resources - 1D and 1E as references for reminding themselves of the names of the ten psalm types.

Closing

If you used either Psalm 95:1-7 or Psalm 100 for the opening prayer, check your church's hymnal to find a familiar hymn based on one of these psalms. If you or someone in the group is able to lead the group in singing, this would be a prayerful, celebrative way to conclude the session.

or

Instead of singing, read in unison the hymn you have chosen.

or

Sing the doxology. It is likely all the members of the group will know the words to this hymn and will not need a hymnal.

Supplementary Readings

Out of the Depths, Chapter 1 and Appendix B.

Bible Dictionary article on Psalms.

Introductory articles on Psalms from one or more study Bibles.

Looking Ahead

In Part 2 we will be working with Psalms as prayers and poetry. Ask the participants this week to pay attention to their own prayers and the prayers of others. Encourage them to notice the names and/or titles by which God is addressed in these prayers.

Arrange to have a copy of the Hebrew Scriptures at the next session to illustrate the nature of acrostic poetry. Psalm 119 will serve as a good example.

In activity #1 in Exploring the Scripture in Part 2 it is suggested that a volunteer present a five minute minilecture on the importance of names in the Old Testament and the significance of God's name. A Bible dictionary and pages 140-145 in *Out of the Depths* will provide helpful information.

Opening Prayer . . . Psalm 95:1-7

O come, let us sing to the LORD;

    let us make a joyful noise to the rock of our salvation!

Let us come into his presence with thanksgiving;

    let us make a joyful noise to him with songs of praise!

For the LORD is a great God,

    and a great King above all gods.

In his hand are the depths of the earth;

    the heights of the mountains are his also.

The sea is his, for he made it,

    and the dry land, which his hands have formed.

O come, let us worship and bow down,

    let us kneel before the LORD, our Maker!

For he is our God, and we are the people of his pasture,

    and the sheep of his hand.   Amen.

455^a
The Psalms^b

BOOK 1^c
(Psalms 1-41)
Psalm 1

1 Happy are those
  who do not follow the advice of the
    wicked,
  or take the path that sinners tread,
    or sit in the seat of scoffers;

2 but their delight is in the law of the LORD,
    and on his law they meditate day and night.

d
3 They are like trees
    planted by streams of water,
  which yield their fruit in its season,
    and their leaves do not wither.
  In all that they do, they prosper.

4 The wicked are not so,
    but are like chaff that the wind drives away.

5 Therefore the wicked will not stand
    in the judgment,
  nor sinners in the congregation
    of the righteous;

6 for the LORD watches over the
    way of the righteous,
  but the way of the wicked will perish.

Psalm 2

1 Why do the nations conspire,
    and the peoples plot in vain?

2 The kings of the earth set themselves,
    and the rulers take counsel together,
    against the LORD and his anointed, saying,

3 "Let us burst their bonds asunder,
    and cast their cords from us."

4 He who sits in the heavens laughs;
    the LORD has them in derision.

5 Then he will speak to them in his wrath,
    and terrify them in his fury, saying,

6 "I have set my king on Zion, my holy hill."

7 I will tell of the decree of the LORD:
  He said to me, "You are my son;
    today I have begotten you.

8 Ask of me, and I will make the
    nations your heritage,
    and the ends of the earth your possession.

9 You shall break them with a rod of iron,
    and dash them in pieces like a potter's
    vessel."

10 Now therefore, O kings, be wise;
    be warned, O rulers of the earth.

11 Serve the LORD with fear, with trembling

12 kiss his feet,¹ ^e
  or he will be angry, and you will perish
    in the way;
    for his wrath is quickly kindled.
  Happy are all who take refuge in him.

---

¹ Cn: Meaning of Heb. of verses 11b and 12a is uncertain.

455[a]
The Psalms[b]

Psalm 3

A Psalm of David, when he fled from his son Absalom.[f]

1 O LORD, how many are my foes!
    Many are rising against me;

2 many are saying to me,
    "There is no help for you in God." [Selah][g]

3 But you, O LORD, are a shield around me,
    my glory, and the one who lifts up my head.

4 I cry aloud to the LORD,
    and he answers me from his holy hill. [Selah]

5 I lie down and sleep;
    I wake again, for the LORD sustains me.

6 I am not afraid of ten thousands of people
    who have set themselves against me all
        around.

7 Rise up, O LORD!
    Deliver me, O my God!
  For you strike all my enemies on the cheek;
    you break the teeth of the wicked.

8 Deliverance belongs to the Lord;
    may your blessing be on your people! [Selah]

---

a.

b.

c.

d.

e.

f.

g.

1   20

Seven Significant Details

Select one of the topics listed below, which are taken from the notes on Participants' Resource - 1B. Use information in the *Resource Book* and other available resources to prepare a brief report regarding your topic.

a This represents a page number placing Psalms between Job and Proverbs. What is the significance of this placement of Psalms?

b What is the origin and meaning of the title of the book *Psalms*?

c What is the significance of "Book 1"?

d What are the characteristics of Psalms as poetry?

e Comment on the meaning of the footnote.

f This line is the title or superscription of a psalm. What information can you find regarding the psalm titles?

g What does *selah* mean?

Matching Exercise for Psalm Types

Read the lines from Psalms in the left column. Look for the name of a psalm type in the right column that matches the quote. Place the appropriate number in the blank.

Words from Representative Psalms   *Psalm Type*

1. *Great is the LORD and greatly to be praised in the city of our God. His holy mountain . . . is the joy of all the earth.* (Psalm 48:1, 2) ____ Psalm of Thanksgiving

2. *How long, O LORD? Will you forget me forever? How long will you hide your face from me? How long must I bear pain in my soul?* (Psalm 13:1, 2b) ____ Sacred History Psalm

3. *For the LORD is a great God, and a great King above all gods. In his hand are the depths of the earth; the heights of the mountains are his also.* (Psalm 95:3, 4) ____ Psalm of Praise

4. *For God alone my soul waits in silence, for my hope is from him. He alone is my rock and my salvation, my fortress; I shall not be shaken.* (Psalm 62:5, 6) ____ Song of Zion

5. *Make a joyful noise to the LORD, all the earth. Worship the LORD with gladness; come into his presence with singing.* (Psalm 100:1, 2) ____ Wisdom Psalm

6. *Our ancestors, when they were in Egypt, did not consider your wonderful works; they did not remember the abundance of your steadfast love, . . . Yet he saved them for his name's sake.* (Psalm 106:7) ____ Psalm of Trust

7. *In your strength the king rejoices, O LORD, and in your help how greatly he exults.* (Psalm 21:1) ____ Psalm of Lament

8. *Lift up your heads, O gates! and be lifted up, O ancient doors! that the king of glory may come in. Who is the King of glory?* (Psalm 24:7, 8b) ____ Royal Psalm

9. *Unless the LORD builds the house, those who build it labor in vain. Unless the LORD guards the city, the guard keeps watch in vain.* (Psalm 127:1) ____ Enthronement Psalm

10. *O give thanks to the LORD, for he is good; for his steadfast love endures forever.* (Psalm 107:1) ____ Liturgy Psalm

Searching for Psalm Types

With a partner skim two to four of the following psalms to determine which type they represent. Note key words and phrases to help you decide and then write the name of the psalm type on the blank line.

Psalm 1 _____	Psalm 76 _____
Psalm 12 _____	Psalm 87 _____
Psalm 15 _____	Psalm 92 _____
Psalm 20 _____	Psalm 95 _____
Psalm 23 _____	Psalm 105 _____
Psalm 30 _____	Psalm 111 _____
Psalm 42 _____	Psalm 119 _____
Psalm 47 _____	Psalm 121 _____
Psalm 66 _____	Psalm 122 _____
Psalm 72 _____	Psalm 136 _____

Psalm types from which to choose:

Psalms of Lament	**Psalms of Praise**
Sacred History Psalms	**Songs of Zion**
Wisdom Psalms	**Psalms of Trust**
Psalms of Thanksgiving	**Royal Psalms**
Enthronement Psalms	**Liturgy Psalms**

PART TWO

PRAYERS AND POETRY

BACKGROUND FROM THE AUTHOR

We have already indicated that Psalms is a book of hymns and prayers written in the form of poetry. In this session we will focus on these two aspects of psalms. Our attention to prayer will deal only with the words and phrases that the psalmists use to address and describe God. In the next session we will explore in more depth and detail the nature of Psalms as a prayer book for God's people.

I attend many services of worship and meetings where pastors or lay persons lead those gathered in prayer. More often than not I observe that those who offer the prayers use a very limited vocabulary when they call God by name or describe the nature of the divine. Everyone has a favorite name or title for God which he or she repeats over and over again. The most frequently used words and phrases are *O Lord, Dear God, Creator God,* or *Father.* The leaders repeat these words or phrases in every other sentence so that it seems they are using them as a pause in order to think of what to say next. It is a mannerism similar to what others do when they intersperse their speaking with *ah* or *you know* or *I mean.* To me this is not only a distracting habit, but it also suggests that the one who is praying has a very limited view of God.

Although I am annoyed when I hear such a limited vocabulary for addressing the Holy One, I realize that God accepts every prayer that is offered and is not offended by the limited knowledge and the incomplete relationship we may have with our Redeemer. However, I am also convinced that we, and those whom we lead, benefit greatly and are nurtured in mind and spirit when our understanding of and relationship with God are expanded to their greatest potential. Such understanding and relationship are affirmed by the way we speak to and about the One who is our refuge and strength.

As leaders of a Bible study group exploring the topic of prayer in Psalms, we need to be very sensitive and careful in the way we approach the subject. Prayer is a very personal activity. Many persons have developed the habit of faithful prayer over many years. They have cultivated familiar and comfortable ways of speaking to and about God. It is not the purpose of this session to call into question the prayer life of the participants. Rather, we want to affirm people in whatever ways they pray and challenge them to continue to be faithful in their prayers. Our goal is to help the participants see the many ways the psalmists addressed and described God in order that they may have their understanding of God enhanced and their prayer vocabulary enriched. After we skim several psalms searching for words and phrases the psalmists used to address and describe the Holy One of Israel, we will make a composite list that will include up to fifty different names, titles, and metaphors. All participants will most likely notice that their favorite form of address is included. And, they will be challenged to select another word or phrase that is not part of their usual vocabulary and to use it as the basis for a personal prayer to the Lord. I hope that for many participants this will open a door into another realm of understanding and relationship with the Sovereign One.

The other major emphasis in this session is on some of the most common features of Hebrew poetry. We have to be careful not to become too technical about these matters. I find that when we approach the poetry of the psalms as if we were trying to solve a word puzzle, most members of the group enter into the fun of the activity and are not intimidated by an art form with which they are not familiar or comfortable. You will notice in the *Resource Book* that in addition to naming the four different types of parallelism I used other more familiar words (they are in bold face type) to indicate the nature of each type. In order to lead this part of the session successfully it is very important for you to be familiar with each of the types of parallelism. The examples from Psalms in the *Resource Book* should be clear and the Participants' Resource sheet with several examples of each type should reinforce the essential features of each type. You will find Bernard Anderson's comments about the poetic structure of Psalms in *Out of the Depths* (pages 34-36) to be helpful.

The last thing we will explore in this session is the form of acrostic psalms. This type of psalm is introduced briefly in the *Resource Book*. The difficult aspect of the form is that it is only apparent in Hebrew. Therefore, it will be helpful to have a copy of the Hebrew Scriptures available for the group members to see. Psalm 119 is the most striking example. Some translations indicate the Hebrew letter for each of the twenty-two stanzas. If someone in the group has such a Bible or you are able to arrange for one, you will have one additional resource to show.

If any members of your group have brought a King James Version or a Living Bible they will be frustrated during this session. Those with King James Bibles will be able to see the parallelism between one line or verse and another, but they will not be able to see the breaks between stanzas. Those with Living Bibles will not be able to deal with any of the poetic structure of Psalms, since in that paraphrase the psalms are presented in a prose format. It will be important to have additional Bibles for these persons so they can be successful in the activities of the session.

SESSION PLANS

Learning Objectives

It is intended that this session will enable the participants to:

1. Identify a variety of names and titles the psalmists used for God.

2. Write a prayer addressing God by a less familiar name or title.

3. Describe the characteristics of four different types of Hebrew poetry.

4. Find examples in selected psalms of synonymous, synthetic, comparative, and antithetic parallelism.

Resources

The following items will be valuable for leading this session:

A copy of the Hebrew Scriptures

Transparency of Psalm 119 from a Hebrew Bible, overhead projector and screen

A variety of translations and versions of Psalms to show similarities and differences and for members of the group to borrow

Participants' Resources - 2A, 2B, and 2C

Newsprint chart with colored markers

Leadership Strategy

Setting the Stage

1. If there are new members in the group ask them to introduce themselves. You may also want to request that all participants wear a name tag or have a "name plate" at their places.

and

Invite participants to share any discoveries or insights they made while reading the *Resource Book* or the Psalms in preparation for this session. Also ask them to share any questions that emerged. Write these questions on a sheet of newsprint or a chalkboard. Don't take the time to answer them all at this part of the session. At the end of the session check the list. If any have not been answered respond to those that are appropriate and identify those that will be dealt with in a later session. Save the list for future reference.

2. For the opening prayer invite everyone to read or pray antiphonally the selected verses of Psalm 27. Make copies of Participants' Resource - 2A, "Opening Prayer," to guide the group in this activity.

or

If all participants have access to the same translation of Psalms guide them in a unison or antiphonal reading of Psalm 27:1, 4, 5, 11-14.

3. Introduce the part of the session that focuses on words and phrases which we use to address and describe God. Ask the participants to imagine they are to lead a group in an opening prayer or their family in prayer before a meal. Instruct them to write the opening sentence of the prayer. After a minute for writing, invite them to state the word or phrase they used to address God. Write the words and phrases on a sheet of newsprint or chalkboard. Indicate that you will return to the list later in the session.

or

If you are concerned about the amount of time needed for the remaining activities of the session, ask the participants to recall the words or phrases that they most frequently use to address God when they pray. Make a list of these words and phrases for use later in the session.

Exploring the Scripture

1. Present a minilecture on the importance of names in the Old Testament and especially the names for God. Refer to Exodus 3:13-15 where Moses inquires about God's name and Exodus 20:7 which is the commandment regarding keeping God's name holy. Emphasize that knowing someone's name was to know something of the essence of the person. See pages 140-145 in *Out of the Depths* and a Bible dictionary for additional information.

or

Introduce the person selected at the last session to present the minilecture on the importance of names and names for God. Provide about five minutes for the presentation.

2. With the previous two activities as a frame of reference, the group is now ready to skim Psalms to see the wide variety of names, titles, and metaphors the psalmists used to address and describe God. If you have ten or more persons in your group divide the first one hundred psalms among the members. (Psalms 1-100 provide at least fifty ways to address or describe God.) Instruct them to just skim the psalms they have been assigned. They are to find all the names, titles, and metaphors the psalmists use for God and to write them on a piece of paper.

or

If you have fewer than ten members in your group, or if you want to take less time for the skimming and searching, use Participants' Resource - 2B, "Searching for Names, Titles, and Metaphors for God," to guide the group. On the sheet seventeen psalms are listed. Assign each person two or three psalms to find words and phrases used to address or describe God.

and

After about six to eight minutes each person should have found five or more different words and phrases. Take time to create a composite list on a sheet of newsprint or chalkboard. Compare this list with the list created earlier in the session from words and phrases used by the members of the group for their own prayers. It is likely they will find their expressions on the psalmists' list. This should be affirming. In addition, they will notice that the psalmists' list is much larger and includes words and phrases that are not part of their prayer vocabulary.

and

Invite the group members to spend a couple of minutes writing brief prayers of three or four sentences. Encourage the participants to include in their prayer one or two words or phrases from the list which they do not ordinarily use when they pray. After everyone has had time to write a brief prayer, invite those who are willing to offer their prayers. Or, you may decide to save the sharing of these prayers for part of the Closing of the session.

3. Introduce the subject of poetry. Ask a few questions such as those below, but do not take too long for discussion. The purpose of this activity is to involve the group members in thinking about poetry from the perspective of their own experiences.

   Q. What images, impressions, or feelings come to mind first when you hear the words poetry or poem?

   Q. If you were assigned to read poetry what would be your response?

   Q. What do you remember about studying poetry when you were in school?

or

If you are concerned about the amount of time left in the session you can just introduce the concept of poetry with a word association activity. Ask for responses to the first question above.

and

Present a five to seven minute minilecture on Hebrew poetry. Use the information from a Bible dictionary, an article in a study Bible, or pages 34-36 from Anderson's *Out of the Depths* to summarize the essential features of poetry in Psalms. Include a review of the four types of parallelism as presented in the *Resource Book*. Provide time for the participants to search in Psalms for one or more examples of each of the four types. Be flexible about designating verses as one or another of the four types. The purpose of the exercise is to practice looking for the characteristics of each type of parallelism. Spend a few minutes sharing what has been found and comparing notes.

Explain the nature of acrostic poems and especially of the form used in Psalm 119 by first looking at this psalm in an English Bible. Call attention to the fact that there are twenty-two stanzas of eight verses each. The number of stanzas equals the twenty-two letters in the Hebrew alphabet. If you have been able to arrange for a copy of the Hebrew Scriptures, show the group the page that includes the beginning of this psalm. Members of the group should be able to see how each verse in a stanza begins with the same letter.

If you have the materials and equipment available make an overhead transparency to show how the eight verses of each stanza begin with a designated Hebrew letter, in alphabetical order.

and

Invite the participants to reflect on the activities of the session. What did they discover? What surprised them? What questions remain unanswered? How will they approach their reading of Psalms this next week?

Closing

Participants' Resource - 2C, contains a choral reading of Psalm 103. Assign the parts quickly and then do the choral reading.

and/or

Find a hymn in your church's hymnal based on Psalm 103 and read or sing it as your closing prayer.

and/or

Invite the group members to share the prayers they wrote earlier in the session. Be clear in your directions that no participants should feel pressured to share their prayers if they prefer not to. Do not go around the circle, but allow for spontaneous sharing by those who feel so motivated.

Supplementary Readings

Out of the Depths, "The Name of God," pages 140-145 and "The Psalms as Prayed Poetry," pages 34-36.

Bible Dictionary articles on Psalms.

Introduction article on Psalms in a Study Bible.

Looking Ahead

In item #1 in Exploring the Scripture in Part 3, it is suggested you or a volunteer present a minilecture on the development of Psalms as part of the canon. See the activity for details.

Opening Prayer . . . Psalm 27

The LORD is my light and my salvation; whom shall I fear?

The LORD is the stronghold of my life; of whom shall I be afraid?

One thing I asked of the LORD, that will I seek after:

to live in the house of the LORD all the days of my life,

to behold the beauty of the LORD, and to inquire in his temple.

For he will hide me in his shelter in the day of trouble;

he will conceal me under the cover of his tent;

he will set me high on a rock.

Hear, O LORD, when I cry aloud, be gracious to me and answer me!

"Come," my heart says, "seek his face!" Your face, LORD, do I seek.

Do not hide your face from me.

Do not turn your servant away in anger,

you who have been my help.

Do not cast me off, do not forsake me, O God of my salvation!

If my father and mother forsake me, the LORD will take me up.

Teach me your way, O LORD,

and lead me on a level path because of my enemies.

Do not give me up to the will of my adversaries,

for false witnesses have risen against me,

and they are breathing out violence.

I believe that I shall see the goodness of the LORD

in the land of the living.

Wait for the LORD; be strong, and let your heart take courage;

wait for the LORD!   AMEN!

Searching for Names, Titles, and Metaphors for God

Select two or three of the following psalms and skim them, searching for all the names, titles, and metaphors used to address or describe God. Write the words and phrases in the spaces adjacent to each psalm.

Psalm 3

Psalm 7

Psalm 18

Psalm 24

Psalm 27

Psalm 28

Psalm 46

Psalm 47

Psalm 59

Psalm 68

Psalm 80

Psalm 84

Psalm 86

Psalm 89

Psalm 91

Psalm 94

Psalm 95

A Choral Reading . . . Psalm 103

Group 1:   Bless the LORD, O my soul,
             and all that is within me, bless his holy name.

Group 2:   Bless the LORD, O my soul,
             and do not forget all his benefits—

Reader 1:   who forgives all your iniquity,

Reader 2:   who heals all your diseases,

Reader 3:   who redeems your life from the Pit,

Reader 4:   who crowns you with steadfast love and mercy,

Reader 5:   who satisfies you with good as long as you live

Reader 6:   so that your youth is renewed like the eagle's.

Group 1:   The LORD works vindication and justice for all who are
             oppressed.

Group 2:   He made known his ways to Moses, his acts to the people
             of Israel.

Group 1:   The LORD is merciful and gracious,
             slow to anger and abounding in steadfast love.

Group 2:   He will not always accuse, nor will he keep his anger forever.

Group 1:   He does not deal with us according to our sins,
             nor repay us according to our iniquities.

Reader 1:   For as the heavens are high above the earth,

Reader 2:   so great is his steadfast love toward those who fear him;

Reader 3:   as far as the east is from the west,

Reader 4:   so far he removes our transgressions from us.

Reader 5:   As a father has compassion for his children,

Reader 6:   so the LORD has compassion for those who fear him.

All: For he knows how we were made; he remembers that we are dust.

Group 1:   As for mortals, their days are like grass;
             they flourish like a flower of the field;

Group 2:   for the wind passes over it, and it is gone,
             and its place knows it no more.

Group 1:   But the steadfast love of the LORD is from everlasting to
             everlasting on those who fear him, and his righteousness
             to children's children,

Group 2:   to those who keep his covenant
             and remember to do his commandments.

Group 1:   The LORD has established his throne in the heavens,
             and his kingdom rules over all.

Group 2:   Bless the LORD, O you his angels, you mighty ones
             who do his bidding, obedient to his spoken word.

All: Bless the LORD, all his hosts, his ministers that do his will.
             Bless the LORD, all his works, in all places of his dominion.
             Bless the LORD, O my soul.   AMEN

PART THREE

PRAYER BOOK FOR GOD'S PEOPLE

BACKGROUND FROM THE AUTHOR

In this session we pick up the previous emphasis on the psalms as prayers. We will explore in some depth the development of Psalms as a prayer book for God's people Israel, for the early church, and for the church today. There is a great deal of material in this chapter, which means that if you have only one hour for your study session you will have to make some adjustments. One adjustment is to schedule an additional meeting for the activities included in the second half of this session plan. Another adjustment is to decide which activities in "Exploring the Scripture" you can accomplish in the time available.

The first section of the *Resource Book* for this part, "Prayer Book for the People of Israel," presents a succinct overview of a large portion of history. This information will be reviewed in the first part of the session. Thus, it is necessary that you or a member of the group do some background reading to become familiar with the development of Psalms in Israel's worship during the Exile and afterwards. In addition to articles in Bible dictionaries, encyclopedias, and study Bibles, Chapter 1 in *Out of the Depths* will be helpful for this purpose.

There are several issues which may arise in the course of this session about which you should be alerted. These include: 1) The use of psalms in corporate worship in contrast to their use for personal devotions, 2) the use and interpretation of Psalms by the New Testament writers, and 3) the relationship of matters which are presented in Psalms to their fulfillment in the New Testament.

On page 31 of the *Resource Book* we quoted Bernard Anderson's understanding of the nature of Psalms as devotional literature for a corporate body. This point of view contrasts sharply with the ways Psalms is often used by Christians today. Many of us see the book as a collection of prayers and hymns to be used primarily for personal reading and devotions. Members of the group who either do not understand Anderson or disagree with him on this matter may question his statement. It is helpful to remember that the Hebrews felt that their identity as the people of the covenant was based upon their inclusion in the community of Israel, not upon their own personal relationship with God. Even though many of the psalms are written in the first-person, they are not written by an individual isolated from the faith community; they are written by persons who are solidly connected with the community and thereby intimately related to the Holy One of Israel.

To view Psalms from this perspective does not diminish its potential for nurturing an individual's spirituality. Just the opposite is true. When individuals recognize themselves to be significantly connected and committed to a body of believers (a congregation, denomination, or the world-wide manifestation of the Body of Christ) the power and passion of Psalms has even greater potential for making a difference in their lives. When we read and pray psalms in the silence of our own sanctuaries at home or work, in the hotel or hospital, on the plane or bus, we recognize that we are joined by a great cloud of witnesses as together we lift our prayers to the Almighty.

Another concern may be expressed by some when they search the New Testament for quotes and references to Psalms. They will notice that when psalms are quoted by New Testament writers the words are not the same in the New Testament as they are in Psalms. There is no need to make an issue of this if no one in the group mentions it, but it will be helpful to be prepared to respond to questions if they arise.

The third issue that could lead you and the group astray is the suggestion that what we read in the New Testament is a fulfillment of what the psalmists wrote hundreds of years earlier. In one sense that is true. From a post-resurrection perspective we can often see connections between what happened in Jesus' life, ministry, death, and resurrection and matters to which the psalmists refer. However, to approach the relationship of the Old and New Testaments from this viewpoint can be very misleading. Jesus did not cry out on the cross, *My God, my God, why have you forsaken me?* because the writer of Psalm 22 envisioned a suffering savior being crucified by his enemies centuries later. The psalmist had a profound experience of being abandoned by God because of the enemies he encountered in his own time and wrote out of his own deep personal agony. Jesus uttered the words not because the psalmist "predicted" he would; rather he uttered the words because he had lived with the power and passion of Psalms all of his life and in the midst of his own terrible agony called upon the familiar words to express his own sense of forsakenness.

If the issue is not raised there is no need for you to raise it. On the other hand, if it is raised try not to let it become the dominant focus of the session. Respond as succinctly and helpfully as possible. You will have to tread carefully on this ground because some in the group may have difficulty viewing the connections between Psalms and the New Testament in the way I have suggested.

SESSION PLANS

Learning Objectives

It is intended that this session will enable the participants to:

1. Describe the development of Psalms as a book of the Bible.

2. Identify aspects of selected psalms that provide clues to their use in the worship life of the Jewish people.

3. Find references to psalms in the New Testament and explain the purposes they served for the writers.

4. Recognize the use of psalms in their church's liturgies and locate hymns in the church's hymnal based upon psalms.

5. Incorporate the style and language of Psalms into their own prayers.

Resources

The following items will be valuable for leading this session:

> Hymnals from the church's worship center
>
> Bulletins with last Sunday's or next Sunday's order of service
>
> Bibles with cross-reference notes
>
> Copy of the Revised Common Lectionary
>
> Copies of Participants' Resources - 3A and 3B
>
> Newsprint easel or chalkboard

Leadership Strategy

Setting the Stage

1. Invite members of the group to share their discoveries from the week's reading in the *Resource Book* and Psalms. Spend a minute or two affirming what individuals share with the group. Ask the participants to state the questions that have arisen during the week. Write these on a sheet of newsprint or chalkboard so they are visible for everyone and determine when to respond to them. Save the list for future reference.

2. The opening prayer[1] for this session will take about five minutes. There are some very specific steps to follow in order for the activity to be successful. We will read and pray, individually and as a whole group, Psalm 63:1-4, which is presented in the Good News Bible translation on Participants' Resource - 3A, "Opening Prayer."

   a After a brief introduction on the background of the psalm, read the verses one line at a time. Invite participants to repeat each line in unison after hearing it. Encourage them to listen for words of the psalm that may be their own personal prayer at the moment.

   b After reading and repeating all the lines, invite participants to select one line or verse to be the focus of their prayers. Allow about twenty to thirty seconds for this.

   c Then ask them to focus on the words they chose and to etch these on their memories, so that when they close their eyes they will be able to repeat them from memory.

   d Allow about a minute for the members of the group to repeat their lines or verse silently, prayerfully.

   e Then invite participants to speak their lines or verses aloud, one at a time. Alert them that it is acceptable for more than one person to speak at a time and it is okay to repeat lines or verses shared by others.

   f To close, invite everyone to pray the psalm in unison.

---

1 This is one of the sixty Bible reading and praying activities in the book, *Meeting God in the Bible: 60 Devotions for Groups*, by Donald L. Griggs and published by The Kerygma Program.

(or)

To shorten this activity begin by asking each person to read Psalm 63:1-4 silently. Then have the group members read aloud the lines or verses that are most meaningful to them. Conclude by praying the passage in unison. Following the prayer, indicate that you will only be able to deal with some of the highlights that are presented in the *Resource Book* for this session. Suggest that members of the group may want to reread Part 3 after they get home.

Exploring the Scripture

1. Introduce the member of the group who prepared during the week to present a minilecture on the historical information regarding the development of Psalms as one of the books to be included in the Hebrew and Christian Scriptures or give the presentation yourself. Use one or more of the resources suggested in the Supplementary Readings to prepare the presentation. Some important points to cover include:

   • Ezra 1-3, especially 3:10-13, which provides some clues regarding the place of Psalms at the time of the return from Exile.

   • Psalms as a part of the worship life of the Jews, with brief references to Psalm 24 as a liturgy for entering the sanctuary, Psalm 81 as a part of the celebration of the festival of booths, and Psalm 121 as a liturgy of blessing of the pilgrims to the Temple.

   • The essence of Bernard Anderson's quote on page 31 of the *Resource Book*.

   (or)

   If you have some assurance that all the members of the group are doing the necessary reading and preparation for each session, you may be able to engage them directly in a brief discussion of this historical material. Guide your discussion with these or similar questions: *—deal w/history of children of Israel ; used in worship —used by NT writers extensively in quotes/paraphrases*

   Q. What are some reasons for including Psalms in the Hebrew and Christian canon of Holy Scripture?

   Q. From Ezra 3:10-13 what clues do you discern that some form of Psalms was included in the worship of the people after their return from exile? *—sons of Asaph —cymbals; trumpets —King David —responsive singing "For his steadfast love endures forever"*

   Q. In what sense is Psalms a prayer book for the corporate body at worship before it is a prayer book for individual spiritual discipline? *Per Anderson: "The individual is related to God as a member of the covenant community."*

41

3

2. Divide Psalms 1-50 evenly among the members of the group so that each person is dealing with two or more psalms. Their task is to look at all parts of each psalm, including the title and superscription. They are to find all the clues they can regarding the use of the psalm in a worship setting. Pages 28-31 in the *Resource Book* indicate the types of clues for which to look. After six to eight minutes ask the members of the group to share what they have found. The purpose of this activity is not to find all the details in every one of the fifty psalms but to call attention to the internal evidence which suggests that psalms were a significant part of the corporate worship life of the people of Israel.

or

If you are pressed for time you can accomplish the same purpose as the above activity by focusing only on Psalms 3 to 6 and 24. Direct the members of the group to look for the same clues mentioned in the *Resource Book*. In these five psalms you will be able to call attention to the following: *Selah* which is a liturgical direction, the use of musical instruments, the presence of a music director, the use of a song tune, and a liturgy for entering the sanctuary.

3. In the *Resource Book* we call attention to the frequent use of Psalms by many New Testament writers. In this activity the participants will have the opportunity to discover some examples where psalms are quoted in the New Testament and to do some analysis of their use.

Divide the larger group into six subgroups. Assign each subgroup one of the following New Testament books: Matthew, Luke, Acts, Romans, Hebrews, or Revelation. If you have fewer than ten in your study group, do not assign one or two of the books; perhaps Revelation and/or Hebrews. The task of each small group is two-fold: Find at least one quotation of a psalm per member of the group, and analyze the use of the psalm by the New Testament writer. Follow the directions on Participants' Resource - 3B, "Psalms Quoted by New Testament Writers." After about ten minutes of working on the task invite each small group to share at least one of its passages and its analysis with the rest of the group.

or

If you do not have sufficient time to divide into small groups, then lead the total group through two different passages: Beatitudes in Matthew 5:1-11 and Romans 3. Use the Participants' Resource - 3B to complete this activity.

4. Our study of Psalms as the prayer book for God's people would not be complete without an opportunity to see how Psalms is incorporated into the worship life of your own congregation. Distribute a copy of last Sunday's bulletin that contains the order of service. Discuss together the places in the order of service where psalms were included in an explicit way. Try to recall anytime in the prayers or sermon when psalms were alluded to. Be sure to check the hymns that were sung to see if any were based on psalms.

and/or

Distribute a hymnal from your sanctuary to each person. If the book has a special section of psalm hymns or responses turn to it first. Look to see how many hymns there are and how many psalms are included in the collection. Then direct the group to the Scriptural Allusion Index, where there is a listing of all the Bible passages on which particular hymns are based. Check the list of hymns based on Psalms. Call attention to the fact that this is usually the longest list by far for any book of the Bible. Count the psalms to see how many are represented. Ask all group members to skim the list to see if there are any hymns based on their favorite psalms. Also look up some of the hymns to see if any of their favorite hymns are based on psalms.

and/or

If your church's worship follows the Revised Common Lectionary this would be a good time to acquaint the group with the current cycle. If you have only one copy of the lectionary show it to the group and pass it around for everyone to see. If you are able, make copies for each member of the lists of passages for the current month or season, including next Sunday. Read all four passages. Discuss briefly the theme or emphasis that provides a link between all of them. Focus especially on the psalm reading. Ask the group what role it thinks the psalm passage plays in this selection of readings. If you have previously reviewed the lectionary to see which psalms are included and excluded for the three year cycle you will want to share some of your observations and findings.

5. To include this activity you will need at least an hour and a half to two hours for the session. We have spent a lot of time looking at Psalms as a prayer book for the people of Israel, Jesus, the early church, and our church today; but we haven't spent any time selecting and preparing psalms for use in a corporate service of worship.

3

Divide the group into pairs. Direct each pair to work on two tasks as if they were members of a worship planning team for their church. They are to select two to six verses of a psalm to be used either as a call to worship, a call to confession, a prayer before reading the Bible, or an affirmation of faith. Then they are to format the psalm verses for reading or praying by the congregation in unison, responsively, or antiphonally. Depending upon the success of the group and the openness of the actual worship planning team, it may be possible that one or more of the psalm prayers can be incorporated into a liturgy at some future time.

or

Lead the group in the same activity as the previous one, but assign each pair a different psalm from the lectionary for the next several weeks. (Use as many weeks as there are members of the group.)

Closing

Close with the sharing of several of the psalm readings or prayers that were prepared in the previous activity.

and/or

Invite persons to select their favorite hymns based on psalms or hymns based on a favorite psalm and sing several of them.

or

Arrange for someone who is comfortable leading others in singing to line out four to six verses of a psalm by first singing each line solo and then inviting the group to sing the line together. Or, someone can read one verse at a time with the group singing a response which will be a line from the psalm.

Supplementary Readings

Out of the Depths, Chapter 1.

Bible dictionary and encyclopedia articles on worship and prayer in the Old Testament.

Looking Ahead

Locate an audio or video cassette recording of the musical, *Fiddler on the Roof*. Prepare to play the segment with the song "Tradition" for the group during activity #3 in Setting the Stage.

Opening Prayer . . . Psalm 63

O God, you are my God,

    and I long for you.

My whole being desires you;

    like a dry, worn-out, and waterless land,

my soul is thirsty for you.

Let me see you in the sanctuary;

    let me see how mighty and glorious you are.

Your constant love is better than life itself,

    and so I will praise you.

I will give you thanks as long as I live;

    I will raise my hands to you in prayer. Amen.

        (Psalm 63:1-4 from the Good News Bible)

Psalms Quoted by New Testament Writers

Directions: Each member of the group will work in one of six subgroups. Your group will be assigned one of the following books of the New Testament: Matthew, Luke, Acts, Romans, Hebrews, or Revelation. Your subgroup's first task is to use the cross-reference notes at the bottom of the page or in the center margin to find passages where the writer has quoted from Psalms. Try to find as many quotations as there are members of your subgroup. The next step is to transcribe both the New Testament text and the Psalms text in the designated spaces below. Then discuss together in your group the questions below.

New Testament Book _____

Psalms Text: _____   New Testament Text: _____

Questions to discuss:

1. What are the similarities and the differences between the wording of the two passages?

2. How does the New Testament writer use the passage from Psalms?

3. What does the passage from Psalms contribute to the point the New Testament writer is making?

PART FOUR

PSALMS OF SACRED HISTORY

BACKGROUND FROM THE AUTHOR

Sacred history psalms have also been called "psalms of the mighty acts of God" and "salvation history psalms." The five psalms in this category have several characteristics in common. They are all longer than most of the psalms. Even though written in poetic form, they are essentially a narrative of events that has a beginning and an ending. The events of the narrative are presented in chronological order. The five sacred history psalms have strong didactic overtones and were most likely used to instruct the people about their heritage and to help them remember that heritage. The essential content of each of the psalms is the great deeds or mighty acts of God. These great deeds reveal God's love for, judgment of, and deliverance of the people with whom God had established the covenant of faith. The events that comprise the narrative are essential to Israel's own self-understanding, as well as essential to understanding who God is as Creator and Lord of history.

Traditions are stories, ceremonies, rituals, events, or other practices that a family, church, community or nation repeats on a regular basis. Unfortunately, traditions can be repeated without purpose or understanding. One of the educational tasks of the church is to be intentional about informing and nurturing its members regarding the meaning and significance of those practices that are repeated on a regular basis. It is especially important to inform and nurture those who are young or new so that they too will be able to appreciate and participate fully in the important traditions of the church's life.

Several activities are included in Setting the Stage. If you have only an hour for your session you will probably have to omit one or two of these. The important thing is to set the stage for the session by opening with prayer and introducing the importance of history and tradition for understanding who we are as God's people in relation to the past, present and future.

The closing activity will take at least ten minutes. You may be tempted to skip that activity if you are pressed for time. However, it is in this activity that the members of the group will gain the clearest sense of how they personally and corporately are part of the sacred history of God at work in our midst. Try to plan the session so that you will have time for this Closing.

SESSION PLANS

Learning Objectives

It is intended that this session will enable the participants to:

1. Describe in their own words the importance of tradition and story telling as ways to communicate their faith to their children and others.

2. Identify the unique characteristics of the five sacred history psalms.

3. Locate examples of God's mighty acts in several other psalms.

4. Suggest connections between God's wondrous deeds in Psalms and their understanding and experience of God's great deeds in their world.

Resources

The following items will be valuable for leading this session:

> Participants' Resources - 4A, 4B, and 4C
>
> Sheets of newsprint and colored markers
>
> Audio or video cassette recording of the musical, *Fiddler on the Roof*, with the song, "Tradition"

Leadership Strategy

Setting the Stage

1. Introduce the focus of this part with a few comments on two key words: *History* and *tradition*. Speak about history as the events, people, and perspectives that shape the collective memory of a people. We are shaped by the history of our families, the history of the nation, the history of the Christian Church, and the history of God's people Israel. Tradition is the repeated stories, customs and rituals of a

family, a church or a nation that help us to remember important happenings in our past and to celebrate their significance for our present.

2. Introduce Psalm 71 as the focus for our opening prayer. Even though this psalm is classified as a psalm of lament there are several references to God's acts. They are called *righteous acts, deeds of salvation, mighty deeds,* and *wondrous deeds.* Make copies of the selected verses of the Psalm on Participants' Resource - 4A on page 54. Pray the prayer in unison. After praying these verses invite the members of the group to look at the words again in order to select one line or one verse that expresses their personal affirmation of faith and trust in God today. Take a few minutes so that those who are willing can share their selected lines or verses. Remind everyone that it is acceptable to remain silent or to share a line or verse that has already been offered by another person.

or

Direct the participants to read Psalm 71 silently. After a few minutes invite them to select a line or verse. Continue the activity as described above.

3. If you are able to locate a recording of the musical, *Fiddler on the Roof,* play the song, "Tradition." The key lines are:

> And how do we keep our balance? That, I can tell you in one word—TRADITION! Because of our tradition we have kept our balance for many years. Here in Anatevka we have our traditions for everything—how to sleep, how to eat, how to work, even how to wear clothes. For instance, we always keep our heads covered, we wear these little prayer shawls. This shows our constant devotion to God. You may ask how did this tradition get started? I'll tell you . . . I don't know. But it's a tradition. Because of our traditions everyone here knows who he is and what God expects him to do.

After listening to the song briefly discuss these questions:

Q. In what ways does tradition help us to keep our balance in life?

Q. How necessary is it to know the origin of a tradition in order for the tradition to have relevance and meaning for our day?

and/or

Encourage members of the group to think about traditions in their families or church that are celebrated on a daily, weekly, monthly, or yearly basis. Invite several persons to share their traditions and to speak briefly about how these traditions help them keep "their balance."

Exploring the Scripture

1. Indicate that we will be working in some depth with five particular sacred history psalms (78, 105, 106, 135, and 136), and briefly with a number of other psalms. Make a two to five minute presentation describing the key characteristics of sacred history psalms. The material in "Background from the Author" and the section entitled "Meditations upon God's Acts in History" in Chapter 2 of *Out of the Depths* will be helpful in your preparation.

and/or

As a group look at Psalm 78:1-8. This is the only one of the five psalms of this type that has what might be called a "prologue" to the listing of the many glorious deeds of God. In the *Resource Book* three topics were described as part of this prologue: the **purpose** of the teaching, the **content** of the teaching, and the **expectations** of those who hear the story of God's wondrous deeds. List these topics on a chalkboard or newsprint. Ask the members of the group to review verses 1-8 and point out phrases or lines related to each of the topics.

or

If you have time, assign each of three groups one of the topics. Ask the members to spend four or five minutes identifying what they see in the eight verses related to their topics. After they have completed their work invite someone from each group to share with the others what he or she has found. Make a composite list for each topic on a sheet of newsprint or chalkboard.

2. In addition to Psalm 78 four other psalms are included in the sacred history category: 105, 106, 135, and 136. Divide the group into five subgroups. Assign each subgroup one of the sacred history psalms. The small groups are to spend about ten minutes reviewing their psalm and answering the following questions. Print the questions on a chalkboard or distribute copies of Participants Resource - 4B to each person.

> Q. What are the beginning and ending points (events or persons) in the history?
>
> Q. In what other books of the Bible is this period of history covered?
>
> Q. What are some of the connecting links that hold the story together?
>
> Q. What is the essential meaning or significance of this history?

Ask each group to share its findings. Receive the answers for one question at a time, and prepare a composite chart on a sheet of newsprint, a transparency, or a chalkboard.

or

If time is limited and you will not be able to involve the group in the above activity, prepare a chart ahead of time using the format suggested on Participants Resource - 4B. Present a minilecture summarizing the answers to the four questions for the five psalms.

3. Refer to pages 46-48 of the *Resource Book* which suggest that there are elements of sacred history in many other psalms. Assign each person one of the Psalms listed below. They are to review the psalm looking for two things: 1) Words or phrases that are synonyms for "sacred history" (see the highlighted examples in the opening prayer from Psalm 71) and 2) examples of God's wondrous deeds. They will have five to eight minutes for this task. After the suggested time has elapsed, invite everyone to share what he or she discovered. Make a composite list on newsprint or a chalkboard of the findings for each of the two categories. After the list is complete spend a few minutes discussing these two questions.

   Q. What does this list tell us about God and the relationship between God and the created order?

   Q. Which of these gracious deeds of God are representative of experiences of God at work in our world today?

   Psalms to consider: 8, 9, 26, 28, 44, 46, 66, 71, 77, 92, 104, 107, 111, 114, and 145.

or

If your time is limited, focus on two to four of the above psalms and call attention to the synonyms for "sacred history" and the examples of God's acts in that history. Spend a few minutes discussing the two questions stated above.

Closing

1. Call attention to the phrases in Psalm 71 which are printed in bold type on Participants' Resource - 4A: *righteous acts, deeds of salvation, mighty deeds, wondrous deeds,* and *great things*. Distribute copies of Participants' Resource - 4C. Guide the group members in considering "great things" God has accomplished in the five categories listed on the sheet (history of the Christian church, their

denomination, their particular church, their family's life, and their own personal lives). It is not necessary for everyone to fill in the blanks in each section. Provide about three to five minutes for this activity.

and

The items participants wrote on their lists will now be used to create and pray together a litany based on Psalm 136. Notice that this psalm is composed of twenty-six brief statements, each followed by the same response, *his steadfast love endures forever.* Several lines or statements all relate to a specific theme and together form a stanza. There are five stanzas:

1. Opening (1-3)

    For God's steadfast love endures forever

2. God the Creator (4-9)

3. God the Deliverer from Egypt (10-15)

4. God the Protector in Battle (16-22)

5. God the Deliverer from Enemies (23-25)

Verse 26 is a concluding call to give thanks.

The litany will be prayed in two parts. Part 1 will be Psalm 136 itself. Ask someone to read the first line of each verse in the psalm. The group is to respond in unison with the refrain, *God's steadfast love endures forever.* Part 2 of the litany will consist of individuals sharing one statement at a time from the lists they composed in the previous activity. After each item is offered, the whole group is to respond with the same refrain. Be sure to provide all the directions for the litany before beginning, so that there will be no interruption along the way.

or

If you do not have time for the above litany, end the session by just praying Psalm 136 responsively.

Supplementary Readings

Out of the Depths, pages 52-56.

Bible Dictionary articles on sacred history.

Bible commentary on Psalms 78, 105, 106, 135, and 136.

Looking Ahead

The next session will focus on psalms of trust. Encourage group members to look for examples of the psalmists' trust in God as they read and pray selected psalms during the week. Ask them to reflect on this concept of "trust" and to consider reasons for and ways they trust God.

Praying with the Psalmist . . . Psalm 71

In you, O LORD, I take refuge;
>   let me never be put to shame.

For you, O Lord, are my hope, my trust,
>   O LORD, from my youth.

Upon you I have leaned from my birth;
>   it was you who took me from my mother's womb.

My mouth is filled with your praise,
>   and with your glory all day long.

My mouth will tell of your **righteous acts**,
>   of your **deeds of salvation** all day long,
>   though their number is past my knowledge.

I will come praising the **mighty deeds** of the Lord GOD,
>   I will praise your righteousness, yours alone.

O God, from my youth you have taught me,
>   and I still proclaim your **wondrous deeds**.

So even to old age and gray hairs, O God, do not forsake me,
>   until I proclaim your might to all the generations to come.

Your power and your righteousness, O God, reach the high heavens.

You who have done **great things**, O God, who is like you?

I will also praise you with the harp for your faithfulness, O my God;

I will sing praises to you with the lyre, O Holy One of Israel.

>   Amen

Five Sacred History Psalms

| Psalm 78 | Psalm 105 | Psalm 106 | Psalm 135 | Psalm 136 |

What are the
beginning
and ending
points in the
history?

In what other
books of the
Bible is this
same period
of history
covered?

What are
some of the
connecting
links that
hold the
story
together?

What is the
essential
meaning or
significance
of this
history?

God's Wondrous Deeds in My World

Spend a few minutes thinking about God's great deeds in the world through the centuries and in your life. Write an example or two in each of the sections below.

In the history of the Christian Church

> *God . . .*

In the _____(denomination)_____ Church

> *God . . .*

In the __(local)__ Church

> *God . . .*

In my family's life

> *God . . .*

In my life

> *God . . .*

PART FIVE

PSALMS OF TRUST

BACKGROUND FROM THE AUTHOR

No doubt each of us has considered the question, "Whom can you trust?" Can we trust our parents, our spouse, our children, our best friend, the law enforcement agencies, our government, the judiciary, the banking institutions, our accumulated resources, our teachers and pastors, our good health, our financial well being? All of these persons and institutions are, or should be, worthy of our trust. However, most of us have had experiences that caused us to be disappointed and to wonder whether any human being or institution can live up to the level of trust we expect. The psalmists recognized that we could not place ultimate trust in weapons, wealth, idols, false gods, or princes. Only God Almighty, Creator of the universe and Lord of our lives, is completely dependable and worthy of our ultimate trust. The psalmists have a great lesson to teach us if only we are open to learn from them.

It is quite possible that the material in this session will cause some to reflect on their life experiences and to realize that they have placed their trust in persons or institutions who have not been faithful. This may be a painful discovery and cause some negative emotions to be expressed during the Bible study. It is healthy, although uncomfortable, for such emotions to be expressed. You will have to decide the extent to encourage sharing among members of the group. If there is a great deal of mutual support and a level of trust has already developed, the individuals who share personal matters may receive the love, forgiveness, and understanding they need to assist in the healing and restoration of trust. The ultimate goal of the session is that we affirm with the psalmists that God is the One who is ultimately trustworthy and who can be depended upon no matter who has disappointed us and what has happened to us.

5

In dealing with psalms of trust we will discover that we are not working with a pure psalm type. Although some, like Psalm 23, clearly fit the category, there are many psalms of various types that contain expressions of trust. It is therefore important to remember that classifying psalms by type is in many ways an arbitrary process. We should allow persons to group them differently than we do. Whenever there are differences the important thing is to share with one another the rationale for such naming.

One of the activities will focus on Psalm 23. For this activity, as well as others in the session, it will be helpful to have as many translations of Psalms[1] as possible. If you are able to secure a copy of the most recent Jewish translation[2] you will find it to be especially useful. Even though persons in the group will have memorized Psalm 23 in the King James Version, they may gain new insight if they hear the psalm from a different perspective. Encourage group members to bring more than one Bible. During the session invite them to read key verses from their various translations. I hope that everyone will come to appreciate the variety without presuming there is one correct translation.

This is the fifth session in the course. The group members have been together long enough to begin to feel comfortable with one another. They have worked together in pairs and small groups in previous sessions. However, in this session they will need to work quickly and cooperatively in order to accomplish the several tasks they will be given. Also, in the final activity they will be asked to express in their own words an affirmation of trust and faith in God. They should be able to succeed with this task. The value of such an activity is that it helps contemporary people articulate, as the psalmists did, what they believe about God and how much they trust God. Significant affirmation and appreciation will be shown by individuals toward one another when they are able to express what they think and believe. We truly can be a blessing to each other when we offer the insights and understandings which we have received through God's own Spirit at work in our lives.

The activities in this session should not present any of the time constraints experienced in the previous session. However, it is possible that one or more participants will want to spend more time than you planned sharing their experiences, beliefs, and feelings with others in the group. This type of sharing may be more important than other things you had scheduled. Be sensitive to the interests and needs of all the members of the group, however, before you encourage an extended time of personal sharing.

---

1 Suggested translations to have available are: King James Version, Revised Standard Version, New Revised Standard Version, The New Jerusalem Bible, The Revised English Bible, The New International Version, and The Good News Bible.

2 *The Book of Psalms: A New Translation According to the Traditional Hebrew Text*. Philadelphia: Jewish Publication Society of America, 1972.

SESSION PLANS

Learning Objectives

It is intended that this session will enable the participants to:

1. Identify several psalms of trust.

2. Recognize the element of trust present in other psalms of various types.

3. Paraphrase a familiar psalm such as Psalm 23.

4. Express their personal affirmation and prayer of trust in God.

Resources

The following items will be valuable for leading this session:

Several different translations and versions of the Bible

Copies of Participants' Resources - 5A, 5B, and 5C

Newsprint easel or chalkboard

Posters or photographs of shepherds and sheep

Leadership Strategy

Setting the Stage

1. Invite members of the group to share their discoveries from the week's reading in the *Resource Book* and in Psalms. Spend a minute or two affirming these discoveries. Ask the participants to state any questions that have arisen during their preparation. Write these on a sheet of newsprint or chalkboard and decide how to respond to them. Save the list for future reference.

2. This opening prayer activity takes less than ten minutes and is very easy to lead. Invite group members to open their Bibles to the Book of Psalms. It does not matter what psalm they turn to. Ask them to skim through Psalms, going forward or backward from where they opened the book. Their task is to spend five minutes looking for verses that reflect the psalmists' trust, confidence, faith, or hope in God. From these they are to select one to three verses that express their own personal trust and confidence in God. When they find a verse they are to mark it and continue skimming until time is called. When the five minutes have expired, invite persons to read or pray their verses. It is not necessary to identify the

selections by chapter and verse. You might also suggest a unison response such as "Praise the Lord," that members of the group can say together after each person shares his or her verses.

or

If you don't have ten minutes for the above activity, select two psalms of trust such as Psalms 62 and 63. Invite persons to select a verse or two from these psalms that express their affirmation and/or prayer of trust and confidence in God. This will take only a minute or two. Then invite participants to read or pray their selected verses, and after each has shared his or her choices, have the group respond with this line from Psalm 63: *O God, you are my God, I seek you.*

or

Read and pray in unison the selected verses from Psalm 16 that are printed on pages 53-54 of the *Resource Book*.

Exploring the Scripture

1. Divide the group into pairs or triads. Each subgroup will work with a pair of psalms from Participants' Resource - 5A, "Psalms of Trust." The psalms in list A are prayers addressed to God and those in list B are affirmations about God. The directions for the activity are included on the worksheet. After ten to twelve minutes the subgroups should have completed their work. As a total group spend some time sharing findings in response to the five questions.

or

Work as a total group on one pair of psalms. Reflect together on the five questions. If time allows, repeat the activity with a second and third pair of psalms.

2. Psalm 23 is familiar to everyone; many will have memorized it. See if the group can recite the Psalm in unison. Ask the members of the group if they remember when they memorized it. Invite them to describe any memorable experiences with the Psalm that they are willing to share with others.

and

Make a brief presentation about characteristics of a shepherd's care and a host's hospitality in the Hebrew culture in which Psalm 23 arose. You will find helpful information in a commentary, a Bible dictionary, or a Bible encyclopedia. You may also want to display posters or photographs of shepherds and sheep. In the *Resource Book* we call attention to the fact that in addition to being known as the "shepherd's psalm," Psalm 23 is also referred to as the "pilgrim's psalm." Contrast the images for God in verses 1-4 with those in verses 5 and 6. Discuss a few questions such as:

Q. Why do you think this is a familiar or favorite psalm of so many?

Q. How helpful are the images of *shepherd* and *host* for our understanding of and relationship to God today?

Q. How does this psalm reflect your trust in God?

Q. What are some "dark valleys" you have been led through by God?

and/or

Assign the following passages to one or more persons. These texts all use the metaphor of shepherd and/or sheep to communicate something of the relationship between God or Jesus and the people who belong to him. The passages are: Psalms 80:1-7; 95:1-7; 100:1-5; Isaiah 40:1-11; Jeremiah 23:1-6; Ezekiel 34:10-23, 30, 31; Matthew 18:10-14; and John 10:1-28. They are to respond to three questions:

Q. How does this use of the image of shepherd compare with Psalm 23?

Q. What do we learn about the nature of God or the ministry of Jesus from this passage?

Q. What do we learn about the nature of God's people from this passage?

and/or

Distribute copies of Participants' Resource - 5B to guide the writing of a paraphrase for Psalm 23 using contemporary metaphors and expressions that come from our culture. Encourage participants to complete as many lines as they can in five to seven minutes. It is not necessary for them to paraphrase each line. Then spend a few minutes sharing the results. Start with line one and invite any who have a paraphrase to share it. Proceed through the remaining seventeen lines in the same fashion.

3. We suggest in the *Resource Book* that there are many psalms that express trust in God in addition to the ones that are classified as psalms of trust. If you can spend fifteen minutes on this activity you should be able to complete it. We are going to look for psalms that include one or more of the following key words: *trust, trusted, refuge, shelter, rock, fortress, house of the Lord*, and others. The directions for the activity are included on Participants' Resource - 5 C. When all group members have completed their exploration, spend a few minutes in pairs or with the

entire group reflecting on the discoveries and the conclusions they have drawn regarding trust in God. Encourage the participants to take about five minutes to write their own psalm or prayer of trust. Use these prayers or affirmations as part of the Closing for the session.

or

If there is not enough time for individuals to do the necessary exploration of additional psalms, take a few minutes to look at three or four psalms that clearly show a strong emphasis on trust in God. Three suggested psalms with which to work are 31, 37, and 71. Consider using the questions under number 4 on Participants' Resource - 5 C to guide the exploration.

Closing

Invite the members of the group to share their prayers or affirmations of trust with one another. Remember that it is not necessary for every member of the group to share what he or she has written. Allow for persons to "pass" if they want to.

and/or

Sing or read in unison one of the familiar hymns based upon Psalm 23.

Supplementary Readings

Out of the Depths, pages 203-217.

Bible commentary focused on psalms of trust.

Bible dictionary or wordbook on words such as *trust, refuge, shelter, rock, fortress,* and *house of the Lord.*

Looking Ahead

Next week the focus of the session is on psalms of lament. This may be a difficult topic for some members of the group. One of the reasons for placing this topic in the next-to-last session is to allow the participants enough time to develop a level of trust and to be willing to share some of their own laments with one another.

Psalms of Trust

Work with one or two other persons. Select one psalm from list A, a prayer addressed to God, and one from list B, an affirmation about God. Read the two psalms and then discuss the questions below.

A Psalm	B Psalm
4	11
16	27
23	62
26	91
31	121
63	125
131	146

Q. What difference do you notice between the two psalms in terms of whom the psalmist is addressing?

Q. What elements of other psalm types (e.g., lament, praise, thanksgiving) do you find in each psalm?

Q. What acts (actions) of God are mentioned?

Q. What responses of the believer are expressed?

Q. Which specific lines or verses of the psalms would lead you to identify the two as psalms of trust?

Prepare to share your findings with another small group or with the whole group.

Psalm 23 . . . Writing a Paraphrase[3]

The LORD is my shepherd,
   I shall not want.
He makes me lie down
   in green pastures;
he leads me beside still waters;
   he restores my soul.
He leads me in right paths
   for his name's sake.

_____

_____

_____

_____

Even though I walk through
   the darkest valley,
   I fear no evil;
for you are with me;
   your rod and your staff—
   they comfort me.

_____

_____

You prepare a table before me
   in the presence of my enemies;
you anoint my head with oil;
   my cup overflows.
Surely goodness and mercy shall
   follow me
   all the days of my life,
and I shall dwell in the house of
   the LORD
   my whole life long.

_____

_____

_____

_____

---

3 From *Meeting God in the Bible: 60 Devotions for Groups*, Donald L. Griggs, © The Kerygma Program.

Expressions of Trust in Other Psalms

1. The leader will divide the Book of Psalms among members of the group.Each person is to work with five to ten psalms. Skim your assigned psalms; don't read them verse by verse. As you skim look for verses that include one or more of the following words or phrases (or their synonyms). The goal is to find as many expressions of trust in as many psalms as possible.

protect(s)	salvation	righteous	trust(ed)	steadfast love
safe	refuge	rock	shelter	strength
fortress	hope	tent	shepherd	house of the Lord

2. Underline, highlight, or otherwise note where these words or their synonyms occur in the psalms you skim.

3. Compare your findings with one other person.

4. Together, reflect on two questions:

    Q. How critical are the key words to understanding the message of the psalmist?

    Q. What do the verses say to you about a believer's trust in God?

5. In the space below write a few verses, using some of the above key words and phrases, and other words that speak of trust, to express your prayer to God or affirmation about God.

PART SIX

PSALMS OF LAMENT

BACKGROUND FROM THE AUTHOR

The Psalms in this part will undoubtedly strike a new chord in the minds and hearts of the group. The *Resource Book* pointedly observes that lament is not a common element of our worship. Indeed, the group may unconsciously react that this category is somehow not appropriate for our devotional life. Here is a communication problem for you to be aware of. The connection between our inner religious experience and the outward airing of our feelings may need to be drawn out.

Who has not felt the complaints expressed in these psalms? But piety may leap too quickly to the conclusion that God will somehow make it all come out right. Honestly, it doesn't all come out that way, does it? Then one is faced with the problem of how to affirm faith when so much of the evidence is negative. And dare we mention this to God?

We are perilously close to the problem of evil, but that issue is too big to tackle in this context. Be ready, however, to go this far: The expectation of an idyllic existence in this world is not only unrealistic; it fails to realize what makes humanity God's people. If nothing ever went wrong, we would not be conscious that it was all right! Being "in the image of God" (Genesis 1:27) means that we can and do make conscious choices. Being "a little lower than God" (Psalm 8:5) means that our choices are not always good. What makes us noble may become an occasion of sin, and then we are driven to learn and understand absolute trust.

At the least, we resent *the prosperity of the wicked* (Psalm 73:3). Or we cringe at the vengeance of Psalm 137:8, 9. It is important for us to get these feelings out in the open (this will need emphasis). And where better than in the compassionate ear of our loving God? When the psalmists uttered their complaints, it opened another way to reach the resolution of their problems.

Our prayers of confession, which are about as close as we usually come to lament, are often routine, sanitized, and couched in flat, religious phrases. We really cannot understand Jacob's wrestling with an angel. In facing God with our laments, however, we are in the best position to find our deliverance. When the psalmist *went into the sanctuary of God,* then he understood that God can handle all our complaints (Psalm 73:15-17).

This also underlines the truth that the individual laments are not to be disconnected from the community laments. The laments of individuals were preserved because the individual was a part of the community. This delicate balance must not be overlooked. I am never alone when I voice my complaint to God, as the psalmists repeatedly declared. I speak as one of the people of God—in Paul's terms, a member of the body of Christ.

One detail that may come up in group discussion is how to understand Jesus' use of Psalm 22 on the cross. The warning has already been directed against taking the psalm as a literal prediction (page 38). It is also important to be sure the group does not think that Jesus' quotation of the first verse of the psalm means he thought that God had really abandoned him. Jesus must have felt, as at no other time, how the weight of human sin separates a person from God. But he also certainly knew the entire psalm and how it moves from lament to affirmation of trust. From the middle of verse 21 the psalm turns to testimony of God's greatness and deliverance: *he did not hide his face from me, but heard when I cried to him* (v. 24).

Awareness of these psalms of lament and acceptance of their guidance for our prayer life will be a healthy experience. This presents a significant task for your leadership. The Closing is the "proof of the pudding" in this part.

SESSION PLANS

Learning Objectives

It is intended that this session will enable the participants to:

1. Describe the distinctive elements of both personal and community psalms of lament.

2. Analyze selected psalms in order to identify the elements of lament in each.

3. Articulate the nature of lament in the context of Psalms as well as in the context of contemporary Christian experience.

4. Consider the appropriateness of including prayers of lament in their own devotional life as well as in corporate worship.

Resources

The following items will be valuable for leading this session:

A chalkboard or newsprint easel

Several translations of Psalms

Copies of Participants' Resources - 6A, 6B, and 6C

One or more dictionaries with definitions of the word "lament"

Leadership Strategy

Setting the Stage

2 1. Invite members of the group to share their discoveries from the week's reading in the *Resource Book* and in Psalms. Spend a minute or two affirming what individuals share with the group. Ask the participants to state the questions that have arisen during the week. Write these on a sheet of newsprint or chalkboard so they are visible for everyone and indicate when you will respond to them during this session or the next. Save the list for future reference.

or

You may want to begin with the praying activity that follows and then return for the above time of sharing insights and questions.

no 2. The opening prayer will take about seven to eight minutes. The steps to follow are clearly outlined in Participants' Resource - 6A. Group members are to choose one of the eight psalms, select a line or verse from the psalm to be their focus, and write a prayer prompted by the words of the line or verse.

Distribute copies of the resource sheet. Briefly review the directions so all group members know what is expected of them. Allow about five to six minutes for reading and writing. Then invite those who are willing to share their psalm verses and prayers with the group.

1 Opening Prayer – selections from Ps 51 – pp. 65-66 of Resource Book

or

If you cannot take the time necessary to involve the participants in the above praying activity, select one of the psalm passages on the resource sheet. As a group, read the passage in unison. Then invite group members to select one line or verse from the psalm, write the line or verse on a blank sheet of paper and continue writing a sentence or two as their own prayer prompted by the selected words of the psalm. Invite those who are willing to share their prayers.

or

If you have less time to allot to the opening prayer activity, just select one of the psalm passages on the resource sheet and read it in unison. Psalm 51 will be especially appropriate for this activity.

3. Brainstorm synonyms for lament. Write all of the suggestions on a sheet of newsprint or chalkboard. Remember, brainstorming means getting as many ideas on the board as possible. There are no wrong responses. And this is not the time to discuss any of the suggestions. The purpose of this brief activity is to get the people thinking about this concept of "lament."

and/or

Share a formal definition for lament from your favorite dictionary or the following definition from the *American Heritage Dictionary*.

> lament: (verb) to express sorrow or deep regret, to mourn, to wail or complain
> (noun) an expression of sorrow or mourning, a dirge or elegy

4. Invite members of the group to make a list of some things that cause them to lament. They might begin by reflecting on circumstances in their family, church, community, state, denomination, country, or the world. Ask them to write a few key words or phrases to represent each lament. Take only about three or four minutes for this. Tell them to put their lists aside. Later in the session we will return to these personal laments.

or

If you think the group will work together quickly and comfortably to create a list of laments, take the few minutes necessary to brainstorm a list of laments and write them on a sheet of newsprint or the chalkboard. Be sure to keep the list for another activity later in the session.

Exploring the Scripture

1. Introduce the psalms of lament by reviewing the following information:

   - More than one-third of the Psalms are laments.

   - There are two types of laments: personal and corporate.

   - There are approximately forty-five personal laments and twenty corporate or community laments.

   - The causes of the laments are many (see pages 68-69 in the *Resource Book* for examples).

   - Though the variety among the psalms of lament is great, there are common characteristics shared by all the laments.

   or

   If the members of the group are faithful in their reading of the *Resource Book* and Psalms, ask questions to elicit the above information instead of making a presentation.

2. Review this activity and the following one. If you do not have time for the whole group to work together on both personal and community laments, divide the group in half. One half can analyze the elements of a personal lament in Psalm 13; the other half can identify the elements of a communal lament in Psalm 80. Have the groups share the results of their work with each other.

   Ask members of the group to turn to pages 71-72 of the *Resource Book* and review the five elements present in most personal psalms of lament. Comment briefly on each of the elements. Then use Psalm 13 as an example. Work as a group to identify the five elements of personal laments in this psalm. Call attention to the key words and verses that represent each of the elements.

   The key words and verses as I see them are:

   - *LORD*, in verse 1 and *O LORD, my God* in verse 3 are the **invocation** or **address to God**.

   - The four statements that begin *How long . . .* in verses 1, 2, 3b, and 4 **lament** the psalmist's personal condition.

- *Consider and answer me . . . give light to my eyes* in verse 3 is clearly a **petition** to God.

- Verse 5 is an expression of **trust**.

- Verse 6 is an expression of **praise**.

3. Next, explore community psalms of lament. Have participants turn to pages 73-75 of the *Resource Book* to review the six elements present in most of these psalms. Comment briefly on each of the elements. Then use Psalm 80 as an example. Have the group identify the elements of a community lament in this psalm. Call attention to the key words and verses that represent each of the elements.

The key words and verses as I see them are:

- Verse 1 is an **address to God**. This is the only psalm of community lament where the invocation, or address to God, is so specific.

- **Laments** of the community appear in verses 4-6, 12, 13, and 16.

- There is evidence of **remembering God's past actions** in verses 8-11.

- **Words of affirmation** are not as clearly present in this psalm as in others.

- The petitions of the psalmist are prefaced with words such as *restore us, turn again, look, have regard, let your hand be upon,* and *let your face shine.*

- There is no expression of **praise** in Psalm 80. However, there is a **vow** in verse 18.

- The Psalm includes a refrain which appears three times, verses 3, 7, and 19.

4. Now that the participants are familiar with the characteristics of individual and corporate laments they should be able to work independently to identify the elements of laments that are present in several additional psalms. Divide the group into pairs. Distribute Participants' Resource - 6B and review the directions. After about ten minutes for this exploration provide another ten minutes for comparing notes and reflecting on insights gained from the activity.

both sides

Closing

As a result of the previous activities the participants should have clearly in mind the five elements of personal laments and the six elements of community laments. Using these elements as an outline, and the concerns giving rise to laments that were identified in Setting the Stage, the members of the group are to write their own prayers of lament. Distribute copies of Participants' Resource - 6C for this activity. Provide about five to seven minutes for writing. The prayers need not be long; one sentence to represent each element will be sufficient. (Remind group members that every lament of the psalmist did not contain all of the elements we have identified.) After time for writing, invite those who are willing to share their prayers as the whole group listens prayerfully.

or

Instead of having individuals write prayers of lament, ask participants to work in small groups of two to four persons. Their task is to write a corporate lament that may be used in the Sunday liturgy in lieu of the usual prayer of confession. The prayers they write should reflect some of the situations present in the church, community, state, nation, or world. They will have identified some of these reasons for lamenting earlier in the session. Conclude with each small group praying its lament in unison.

Supplementary Readings

Out of the Depths, Chapter 3.

Bible Dictionary article on lament.

Looking Ahead

Invite participants to pay close attention to next Sunday's service of worship. Ask them to notice all of the times when there is any element of praise in hymns, anthems, prayers, Scripture, or responses during the service.

Psalms of Lament for Personal Meditation

Select one of the following psalm passages to read. Read the passage slowly and prayerfully. Ponder the words. Focus on those words that express your thoughts and feelings today. Select one line or verse that is especially meaningful to you.

1. Psalm 6:1-10   "My eyes waste away because of my grief."*

2. Psalm 13:1-6   "How long, O LORD? Will you forget me forever?"

3. Psalm 41:1-12   "Even my bosom friend . . . has lifted the heel against me."

4. Psalm 51:1-17   "Have mercy on me, O God, according to your steadfast love."

5. Psalm 71:1-21   "I will come praising the mighty deeds of the Lord God."

6. Psalm 85:1-13   "Will you not revive us again so that your people may rejoice in you?"

7. Psalm 90:1-17   "For a thousand years in your sight are like yesterday when it is past."

8. Psalm 119:81-88   "My soul languishes for your salvation; I hope in your word."

Read the line or verse as your prayer, then write the line or verse on a separate sheet of paper. Continue writing for three to four minutes. Don't worry about what to write; the words will come easily as you reflect on the words of the psalm and their meaning for you.

---

* These brief quotes from the Psalms are from the NRSV Bible.

Analyzing Psalms of Lament

Psalms of lament, both personal and communal, include the following elements, although not all laments have all these elements, nor are they always in the same order.

1. Invocation or address to God.
2. Lament.
3. Remembering God's past action.
4. An expression of affirmation or trust in God.
5. Petition or supplication.
6. Expression of praise or vow to praise.

Work in pairs. Select two or three of the psalms listed below to analyze. Identify which of the six elements are present. Also indicate whether they are individual or community laments. Be prepared to share and compare notes/findings with the whole group.

5, 17, 22, 35, 38, 39, 42, 44, 47, 58, 71, 74, 79, 80, 83, 85, 88, 90, 140, and 143

Psalm _____ is a personal ___ community ___ lament

   Elements Present   Key words and/or verses

   1.

   2.

   3.

   4.

   5.

   6.

Psalm _____ is a personal ____ community ____ lament

Elements Present

Key words and/or verses

1.

2.

3.

4.

5.

6.

Psalm _____ is a personal ____ community ____ lament

Elements Present

Key words and/or verses

1.

2.

3.

4.

5.

6.

Writing a Prayer of Lament

Using the concerns identified earlier in the session, the elements of lament psalms, and the form below, write a prayer of lament. Write either a personal lament or a corporate lament.

Invocation/address to God . . .

My lament . . . (for myself or for the community)

I remember God's past mighty acts . . .

I express belief/trust in God . . .

I petition God to . . .

I make a vow to God and/or I praise God . . .

PART SEVEN

PSALMS OF PRAISE

BACKGROUND FROM THE AUTHOR

Here we are at the end of this course of study in which we have been discovering the rich resources of the Book of Psalms. It is entirely fitting that this last chapter look at the Psalms of Praise. You and your group will certainly want to join with the psalmists in praise.

Several matters may be mentioned to support your study and to anticipate details that may arise in the session. The section on praise in books other than Psalms is supplemental but very important. It demonstrates how essential this response to God is in all the Scriptures. Martin Luther referred to Psalms as a "Bible in miniature . . . all things which are set forth more at length than the rest of the Scriptures are collected into a beautiful manual of wonderful and attractive brevity."

In the case of "praise," we may reduce the focus to one word, "Hallelujah." This word is formed from two roots which are translated "Praise the LORD!" (The "jah" is a short form of "Yahweh.") It occurs 29 times in Psalms 104-150. Psalms 113-118 are known as the "Hallel" Psalms and have been used in the Passover celebration. In translating the word into Greek, the "h" sound is lost, and this form has passed into English as "Alleluia." "Hallelujah" occurs four times in Revelation 19, and verse six is the source of Handel's "Hallelujah Chorus."

Here again the close connection between personal praise and worship by the assembly is plain. "Hallelujah" is not only an expression of corporate worship; it is an imperative to the participating persons to join in praise. It was used in early church liturgy, perhaps as encouragement to the people to serious participation in the service.

The word is popular today as a response to religious feeling. At least that is the biblical intent of the word. It should never be uttered lightly. It should be an expression of deep spiritual experience. After all, one is addressing Almighty God, and that is a most serious matter.

Now several footnotes: The Session Plans remind you about the value of using several translations. This is important for at least three reasons. (1) All translation is to some extent interpretation, and the use of various versions is in effect employing commentary. (2) This use will move the group from tolerance of the versions used by others to appreciation of their value. (3) Striking phrases will appear that will illuminate and make memorable the text.

In Setting the Stage - #3, remember that you are a fallible leader, one of the learners in the group. There may be some questions for which you have no answers and other questions that should be the subject of another session or a whole new study on Psalms. Admit where you have no answers and assure the group members that it is not necessary always to have conclusive responses to every question. You may also find it necessary to defer some answers because there is not enough time.

This is the end of this course of study. Praise is the most appropriate subject that could be used with this session. Try to bring both the session and the course to a climax in a mode of praise.

SESSION PLANS

Learning Objectives

It is intended that this session will enable the participants to:

1. Recognize the aspect of praise in many psalms.

2. Identify the key characteristics of psalms of praise.

3. Use their church's hymnal to find hymns of praise and make connections to psalms of praise.

4. Experience the joy of praising God guided by one or more psalms.

5. Bring closure to the seven week discovery of Psalms.

Resources

The following items will be valuable for leading this session:

Hymnals used in the congregation's worship

Copies of the previous Sunday's order of service

Chalkboard or newsprint easel

Copies of Participants' Resources - 7A, 7B, 7C, and 7D

Simple musical instruments: horn, tambourine, cymbals, and stringed instruments.

Leadership Strategy

Setting the Stage

1. The opening prayer will take about seven or eight minutes. We included this activity in Session 5. Invite group members to open their Bibles to the Book of Psalms. It does not matter which psalm they turn to. They are to skim through Psalms, going forward or backward from where they opened the book. The task is to skim, not to carefully read complete verses. As they skim, participants are to look for verses that express praise to God. From these verses members of the group are to select two to four verses that will serve as their own personal prayer of praise. They can mark the places where they find these verses while they continue to skim for more verses.

As soon as the directions are understood tell the participants to start skimming. Keep track of the time. Allow just four or five minutes. Everyone will be able to find something in that amount of time. Then invite group members to read the verses they selected. There is no need to identify these by psalm and verse numbers. After a person has read his or her verses the whole group is to respond in unison with a response you have selected. With the topic of praise, an appropriate response is *Praise the Lord*! This is a favorite response of the psalmists.

or

Read or pray in unison a psalm of praise. If everyone does not have the same translation you can print the psalm on newsprint or distribute photocopies of it. This may be a good time to introduce the group members to a translation of Psalms which is a little different than the one with which they are most familiar.

(Two examples are *The New Jerusalem Bible* or *The Holy Scriptures* from the Jewish Publication Society.)

and/or

Sing one or two stanzas of familiar hymns of praise based on psalms.

2. Review last Sunday's liturgy using bulletins with the order of service. Ask participants to recall all of the occasions of praise during the service. There may be some differences of opinion. That will provoke a discussion of why individuals thought particular items could be seen as examples of praise.

3. Invite members of the group to share their discoveries from the week's reading in the *Resource Book* and Psalms. Spend a minute or two affirming what individuals share with the group. Ask the participants to state the questions that have arisen during the week. Write these on a sheet of newsprint or chalkboard.

Review the lists of questions from the previous six sessions. Notice how many have been answered. This is the time to respond to any questions that remain unanswered. Answer them as quickly as possible. When satisfying answers cannot be formulated, and since this is the last session of the course, encourage participants to continue their study and exploration of Psalms.

Exploring the Scripture

1. One would expect some form of the word *praise* to appear frequently in Psalms. There are one hundred thirty-eight such verses. On the other hand, it may be a surprise to discover that some form of the word is also present in seventy-six verses in nineteen other books of the Hebrew Scriptures. In this activity we will spend time with six passages which feature praise.

Divide the group into six smaller groups. Assign each small group one of the following passages: Exodus 15:1-21; 2 Chronicles 5:1-14; Ezra 3:1-13; Isaiah 25:1-12; Isaiah 42:1-13; and Daniel 6:1-16. Distribute copies of Participants' Resource - 7A, "Praise in Other Hebrew Scriptures," to guide the small groups in their exploration. The questions for each group to discuss are listed on the resource sheet.

After the small groups have completed their work, ask each to share the results of its exploration with the others. Receive responses from all groups to one question at a time.

or

If you have limited time for this session (less than ninety minutes), you may want to have the whole group work together on two or three of the passages. Discuss responses to each of the three questions for a passage before moving to the next one.

2. Turn to pages 83-86 in the *Resource Book,* and review the characteristics of psalms of praise. These are the characteristics that the group members will seek to find in the psalms with which they will work. Use Psalm 30 as a basis for identifying these characteristics. (Psalm 30 was not included among the Basic Bible References because it is identified as a psalm of thanksgiving by the editors of the *New Oxford Annotated Bible: NRSV.* However, there is great similarity between psalms of praise and psalms of thanksgiving and Psalm 30 does have the characteristics of a psalm of praise.) With the whole group, take time to call attention to the following:

   • Address to God . . . *I will extol you, O LORD.* (v. 1)

   • A past distress . . . *I cried to you for help, and you have healed me.* (v. 2; see also v. 5)

   • A plea to God . . . *To you, O LORD, I cried, and to the LORD I made supplication.* (v. 8)

   • Recalling God's gracious deeds . . . *You have turned my mourning into dancing.* (v. 11a; see also vs. 3, 7, and 11 b, c)

   • Ascription of praise . . . *O LORD my God, I will give thanks to you forever.* (v. 12)

3. Distribute copies of Participants' Resource - 7B, "Exploring Psalms of Praise," to guide members in exploring selected psalms of praise. Now that they are familiar with the characteristics of these psalms, they should be able to identify these characteristics readily. If you have twenty or more members in your group, divide them into ten small groups. Ask each small group to work with a different psalm of praise. (Have the group select from Psalms 33, 100, 111, 113, 114, 145, 146, 147, 149, and 150.) The group members are to use the worksheet to explore their psalm. Remind them that particular psalms may not have all of the characteristics, and they may not be in the order presented above.

   After the groups have finished their work, spend a few minutes reflecting together on their discoveries. You may want to guide the reflection with questions such as:

Q. Which characteristics are present and which are missing in your psalm?

Q. What did you learn about the psalmists' understanding of or belief in God through these psalms of praise?

Q. When you praise God which of these elements are most often present in your prayers?

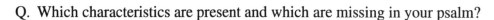

or

If there is not enough time to work in small groups, you may want the whole group to work together on two or three of the psalms. Refer all members to Participants' Resource - 7B and remind them of the characteristics of psalms of praise.

or

If you have a small group, assign individuals particular psalms and refer them to Participants' Resource - 7B. Remind them of the characteristics of psalms of praise and invite them to look for these marks in their assigned psalms.

4. If you have limited time available for your session you may decide to omit this activity. Or, you may be able to schedule an additional session where this activity is featured. As we have noted before, many hymns are based upon Psalms. Distribute a hymnal to each participant. Spend a few minutes with the hymnals to become acquainted with hymns whose origins are found in Psalms. First, look in the topic index to see if there is a section focused on praise of God or praise of Jesus Christ. Skim the list to see how many hymns there are and which ones are familiar to members of the group. Next, check to see if there is a scriptural allusion section in the index. If so, look to see how many of the fourteen psalms of praise are included in the list. How many of these hymns are familiar? Sing the first stanza of one or two. Finally, turn to the alphabetical index to see how many hymns begin with the word praise or include praise in their title.

or

In lieu of involving the group in exploring the hymnal, invite the music director, organist, or choir director to make a brief presentation about hymns of praise and hymns based upon psalms of praise. It is important for each participant to have a hymnal and to spend some time singing the first stanzas of several hymns.

5. Using Participants' Resource - 7C, "Writing a Psalm/Prayer of Praise," guide the members of the group in writing a psalm or prayer of praise which includes the

five elements described earlier. Encourage them to write one sentence for each of the five elements. Most participants should be able to write these sentences in about ten minutes. After the time for writing invite those who are willing to share their psalm/prayers of praise. Or, you may want to save these psalm/prayers to be included as part of the Closing.

Closing

1. Before bringing the session and the course to a close spend a few minutes guiding the members of the group in reflection on the experience of the course and their discoveries regarding Psalms. The discussion could be guided by questions such as those that follow. However, the best questions will be the ones you develop from your experience of working with the group.

   Q. What were some highlights for you in this course on Psalms?

   Q. What new insights do you have regarding Psalms?

   Q. What new approaches to reading the Bible and praying have you discovered in this Bible study course?

   Q. What are some remaining questions that you hope to explore regarding Psalms?

   Q. What is your favorite type of psalm?

2. If prayers of praise were written earlier and not shared at that time you will want to include them as part of the Closing. You will have to decide whether to do this first or the activity with Psalm 150 that follows.

and

To bring closure to this session on psalms of praise and on the whole course, lead the group in reciting Psalm 150 and doing the suggested actions that are described on Participants' Resource - 7D, "Praise the Lord . . . Psalm 150." You will need to arrange for some simple musical instruments. The best source may be the nursery or preschool classes in your church. Check with the teachers of those groups to see if they can help you.

and/or

Sing a hymn of praise such as: "All People that on Earth do Dwell" (Psalm 100), "Praise the Lord You Servants of the Lord" (Psalm 113), "I'll Praise My Maker" (Psalm 146), or "Give Praise to the Lord" (Psalm 149).

Supplementary Readings

Out of the Depths, pages 39-51.

Looking Ahead

There is no session to prepare for next week. However, you may want to follow up with the participants in several weeks to discuss together what, if any, continued reading and praying with the Psalms they are doing.

Praise in Other Hebrew Scriptures

A. Work with a small group of people. Each group is to select one of the following passages which features praise of God in some form. It will be helpful to look at the context of the passage in order to respond to the three questions listed below.

1. Exodus 15:1-21   "I will sing to the Lord, for he has triumphed gloriously"

2. 2 Chronicles 5:1-14   "It was (their) duty . . . to make themselves heard in unison in praise . . ."

3. Ezra 3:1-13   "And all the people responded with a great shout when they praised the Lord . . ."

4. Isaiah 25:1-12   "O Lord, you are my God; I will exalt you, I will praise your name."

5. Isaiah 42:1-13   "Sing to the Lord a new song, his praise from the end of the earth!"

6. Daniel 6:1-16   "(He got) down on his knees three times a day to pray to his God and praise him . . ."

B. Discuss these three questions:

Q. What appears to be the reason for praising God? What is the setting?

Q. How is God addressed? What name, title, or image of God is used?

Q. What is the form or the means by which the praise is expressed?

Exploring Psalms of Praise

A. Work in small groups. Each group is to select one of the following psalms and find the elements that are present in it.

> Psalms 33, 100, 111, 113, 114, 145, 146, 147, 149, and 150.

B. In the spaces below write the key words or phrases from your psalm which match the different categories.

An invocation or address to God:

The body of the psalm, which includes one or more of the following.

> A past distress:

> A plea for help:

> A remembering of God's gracious deeds:

Ascription of praise:

Writing a Psalm/Prayer of Praise

In the next few minutes compose a psalm/prayer of praise using the outline we have already identified. Write at least one sentence for each of the elements listed below.

An invocation or address to God:

A past distress:

A plea for help:

Remembering of God's gracious deeds:

Ascription of praise:

Praise the LORD . . . Psalm 150[1]

The group is to stand in a circle with room enough between persons to extend arms.

Praise the LORD!	(Shout "Hallelujah")
Praise God in his sanctuary;	(reach out to hold hands)
praise him in his mighty firmament!	(with hands held, raise high)
Praise him for his mighty deeds;	(clap hands)
praise him according to his surpassing greatness!	(clap hands louder)
Praise him with trumpet sound;	(blow horns)
praise him with lute and harp!	(strum on string instruments)
Praise him with tambourine and dance;	(shake tambourine, dance)
praise him with strings and pipe!	(strum on string instruments)
Praise him with clanging cymbals;	(bang cymbals)
praise him with loud clashing cymbals!	(bang cymbals more loudly)
Let everything that breathes praise the LORD!	(speak, "Praise the Lord")
Praise the LORD!	(shout loudly, "Praise the Lord!")

---

1 This activity is from *Meeting God in the Bible: 60 Devotions for Groups*, Donald L. Griggs, The Kerygma Program, © 1992. Used by permission.